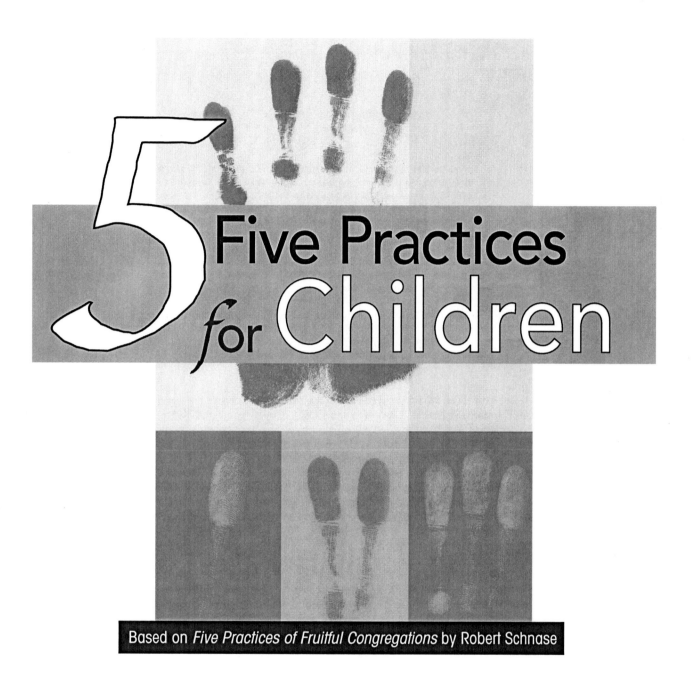

5 Five Practices for Children

Based on *Five Practices of Fruitful Congregations* by Robert Schnase

Rita B. Hays

ABINGDON PRESS
Nashville

Five Practices for Children

Based on *Five Practices of Fruitful Congregations* by Robert Schnase

Scripture quotations in this publication, unless otherwise indicated, are from the Common English Bible, Copyright © 2010 by Common English Bible, and are used by permission.

Scripture quotations noted NRSV are taken from the New Revised Standard Version of the Bible, copyright 1989 by the Division of Christian Education of the National Council of the Churches of Christ in the United States of America. Used by permission. All rights reserved.

The Rev. Dr. Rita Hays, an ordained deacon in the Tennessee Conference, is Associate Pastor for Children, Visitation, Education, and Family Ministries at Connell Memorial United Methodist Church in Goodlettsville, Tennessee. She has served in the local church in the area of Christian Education for over twenty-five years and has led numerous workshops on the district, conference, and national levels for The United Methodist Church. Hays also serves as an adjunct professor at Lindsey Wilson College in Columbia, Kentucky. Dr. Hays is the author of *The Children's Minister* and *The Most Important Space in the Church: The Nursery*, both published by Discipleship Resources, and *All in the Family: Faith Issues for Families Facing Addiction*, published by WestBow Press.

Rev. Hays received her Bachelor of Arts degree from Mercer University, her Master of Religious Education degree from The Southern Baptist Theological Seminary, and her Doctor of Ministry degree from Presbyterian Theological Seminary. She also completed graduate courses at United Theological Seminary and Scarritt College. She lives in Nashville, Tennessee.

ISBN-13: 9781426716423

PACP 00858986-01

Editor: Daphna Flegal
Production Editor: David Whitworth
Production and Design Manager: Marcia C'deBaca
Cover images: ThinkStock

10 11 12 13 14 15 16 17 18 19—10 9 8 7 6 5 4 3 2 1

TABLE OF CONTENTS

1.

Radical Hospitality for Children

Introduction

Third-grader Andrea Coates finds herself in an uncomfortable position one particular Sunday morning. She and her family are visiting a new church, a congregation full of strangers. As Andrea and her family enter the doors, Andrea notices the stares of the greeters, friendly glances that, nonetheless, label them immediately as "visitors" and "outsiders." Andrea nervously twirls the ribbon on her Sunday dress as she watches the ushers warmly greet her family and hand them a bulletin. Suddenly, out of the corner of her eye, Andrea observes an unfamiliar figure approaching her. One of the children of the church, Sylvia Shepherd, runs excitedly toward Andrea, insisting that Andrea and her family come and sit with Sylvia's mom, brother, and herself.

After the introductions are made and while the Shepherd family introduces Sylvia's parents to other church members, Sylvia gets Andrea a children's worship bag, filled with materials appropriate for children in the worship gathering. She also informs Andrea of exactly what is going to happen when it is time in the service for the children's chat, a time when the pastor will talk with the children. Andrea's face shows evidence of fear as she dreads leaving the security of the church pew to make her way to the front, but Sylvia

assures Andrea that she will go with her. She also promises Andrea that she will accompany her to children's worship and introduce her to the teachers and other children.

What would motivate a fourth-grader named Sylvia Shepherd to reach out in Radical Hospitality to a stranger? Sylvia Shepherd belongs to a congregation that has been teaching its members about the practice of Radical Hospitality. Sylvia has learned that Radical Hospitality is going out of one's way to make another person feel welcome. Sylvia has learned Bible stories about this biblical concept from her Sunday school teachers, her children's worship leaders, her family, and her pastor. Children in her congregation have not been excluded from teachings about Radical Hospitality; rather, they have been challenged to fully participate along with other members of the congregation. Ways to practice Radical Hospitality have been taught to the children; so, when the occasion presented itself, Sylvia was prepared, ready, and willing to share.

Seth Miller and the members of his confirmation class prepare a meal for the members of an inner-city church to which the congregation ministers on a regular basis. Seth cannot sleep that evening, however, as he thinks about the children he met and their needs. In the middle of the night, God gives Seth a vision of how to show love to them. Seth decides to enlist the help of his confirmation class to host a party for these children. With his leadership, the class plans the party, invites the children, decorates the inner-city church, secures refreshments, plays games, and provides gifts for each attendee. They extend Radical Hospitality to each child.

What would motivate a sixth-grader to reach out in Radical Hospitality to children very different from those in his church? Like the young boy Samuel, to whom God spoke in the middle of the night, Seth senses a strong call from God to help others. Like the priest Eli, who affirmed the call of Samuel, Seth's pastor took seriously the call of Seth to practice Radical Hospitality.

What is Radical Hospitality?
What does it have to do with children?

Our congregations are filled with children who want to serve their church and their God. All they need is the encouragement of their pastors, Sunday school teachers, parents, church leaders, and congregation. They also need training. They must be taught biblical and practical ideas on how to become hospitable children. Radical Hospitality is not just the gift God graciously pours out upon adults and youth, but also the gift of the Spirit given to children as well. Congregations value and bless children when they guide them toward ways to express Radical Hospitality to others and then grant them the freedom to do so.

Radical Hospitality flows from our understanding of God's grace. God extends grace to all of God's children, regardless of our race, gender, age, or cultural background. God reaches out to each of us, offering us the free gift of salvation. God's grace calls us into a relationship with Jesus Christ. God's grace never gives up on us even when we distance ourselves from God. God is a gracious, loving, generous God. God practices Radical Hospitality! We who seek to be in relationship with our God of hospitality must leave behind our comfort zones for the sake of others. Radical Hospitality demands that we

reach out to those with whom we come in contact, whether they are friend or stranger, and extend the love of Christ. This hospitality requires more than a friendly handshake; it means that we invest in the lives of others in such a way that they are captured by God's grace at work in our lives and their lives. We offer others hope, the hope grounded in our faith in Christ. We offer others joy, the joy that flows from our relationship with our God. We offer others compassion, rather than pity, because we serve a compassionate God. We offer others the kind of hospitality that has been extended to us through our Lord and Savior Jesus Christ.

United Methodists are a people entrenched in the tradition of Radical Hospitality. Throughout our history, the people called Methodists have ministered to the social outcast, to the prisoner, to the poor and needy, and to the hurting. John Wesley envisioned a people who would share the love of Christ through acts of mercy and kindness. Social justice linked with the gospel message transforms lives and generates Radical Hospitality.

Worshipers in the Wesleyan tradition experience the concept of Radical Hospitality in our two sacraments of Baptism and Holy

Communion. Jesus Christ invites all persons to his table of reconciliation. Christ's table is always a place of Radical Hospitality. Persons baptized into the community of believers are welcomed into a fellowship of grace. Infant baptism expresses God's Radical Hospitality toward infants, those who cannot answer for themselves the faith questions of our tradition but who nonetheless are welcomed with open arms by Parent God. When children are invited to the Table, they learn about a God who welcomes all persons regardless of who they are. When they observe the baptism of an infant, they can be reminded of their own baptism, their own ceremony of welcoming into the life of the church. They can also remember that God is always reaching out to each of us with God's grace and love, extending Radical Hospitality to us at every moment of our lives, even to infants who are unaware of God's grace at work. All of these expressions of hospitality are important visible reminders of Radical Hospitality, lessons learned by children who are included fully in the worshiping community. For these reasons, churches should make every effort to include children in the sacraments of Baptism and Holy Communion so that these children can experience Radical Hospitality through these means of God's grace.

Furthermore, Radical Hospitality is tied up with our call to Christian discipleship. At the 2008 General Conference, the delegates adopted a mission statement as a guiding principle for all United Methodists. United Methodists were urged to form disciples of Jesus Christ so that the world would be transformed. Our disciple-making includes helping persons live out their faith as followers of Jesus Christ by practicing Radical Hospitality toward others in the body of Christ and in the world.

Radical Hospitality flows from our understanding of God's grace.

Our teachings about Radical Hospitality through Bible stories and modern-day examples will be more powerfully received by children when they have seen their congregations putting Radical Hospitality into practice. When children are in corporate worship, they observe the actions of those around them. Do they see ushers warmly greeting visitors, including children, and introducing them to other church members or do they see visitors being received in a lukewarm manner? Do their Sunday school teachers welcome them or do they forget their names? Are children invited to take part in mission projects of the church family or do adults lack the patience to work alongside children? Are children allowed to participate fully in all of the events of the church family or do they feel excluded from some areas of church life? Does the community of faith feel like family to children?

How does the congregation welcome strangers who speak a different language or come from a different culture from the majority of the congregants? Would a homeless person be welcomed in the life of the congregation? How would the congregation treat persons whose lives are affected by addictions? Do members reach out to persons with physical and mental challenges? Would they advocate for the rights of persons with mental illnesses to be included fully in the life of the church?

Children are keen observers, and their first lessons in hospitality will come from watching the ways church members practice hospitality. We cannot expect children to take seriously the lessons we desire to teach them about hospitality in the Bible or the examples we give them of ways to practice hospitality in their lives today unless we first live out in congregational life the gift of Radical Hospitality.

Workshop for Lesson One

Encourage the members of your children's ministry team, your Sunday school teachers, and other volunteers in your children's ministry area to gather for a time of teaching and reflection on the ways children in the church may be involved in acts of Radical Hospitality.

Prayer and Welcome

Reflections on John 6:1-14

If your group is large enough, divide into several teams to complete the following exercises and then return as an entire group to share your insights.

Team One:
Pretend you are the young boy with the lunch of five loaves and two fish. Share what you are feeling, seeing, and thinking as you observe Andrew searching the crowd for food to feed the people gathered that day. Write out a conversation between Andrew and the young boy and act it out.

Team Two:
Pretend you are Andrew. You start to hear the grumblings of the mass of people who are getting hungry and are beginning to loudly complain. Share what Andrew might have been thinking and feeling that day as he searched the crowd for some food. Write out a conversation between Andrew and some of the people in the crowd who are tired, hungry, and complaining to Andrew and the other disciples and act out your written conversation.

Team Three:
Pretend you are the young boy returning home to share his story with his family. John's Gospel does not tell us if any of the boy's family members were present with the lad that day, but let's pretend they are waiting at home. Write out a conversation between the child and his family members and act out your written conversation.

Team Four:
Think up a modern-day rendition of the Bible story. Write it out in skit form, in the form of an advertisement, in a television or radio commercial, or in cartoon form.

Bring the teams back together and let each team share. List some of the key components of Radical Hospitality that can be learned from this story.

- This is an example of the way a child practiced Radical Hospitality.

- Radical Hospitality begins when we recognize a need. In this case the people were hungry and Andrew tried to respond by searching the crowd for food.

- Jesus confirms that the offering of this lad is sufficient. Jesus can take our gifts of Radical Hospitality and use them in ways we cannot begin to imagine if we are willing to share.

- Radical Hospitality is risky. It challenges us to leave our comfort zones and step out in faith. In the case of the child in our story, he had to set aside his worries about the reaction of his family to his giving away his lunch. He had to forget about his own hunger so others could be fed.

Affirm the Ways Your Children Now Engage in Radical Hospitality

Ahead of time, find or draw a large picture of a church, heart, tree, or other symbol that represents for your congregation Radical Hospitality. Tape it to the wall.

Place some sticky notes at the table where participants are sitting. Give them two minutes to write down all of the ways the children in your congregation are currently practicing Radical Hospitality. These can be ways practiced by groups of children or by individual children within the church or community. When time is up, have participants come forward and post their sticky notes on the symbol taped to the wall.

Read out what is written on each sticky note. After you read each note, have participants respond with the words "Thanks be to God" as an affirmation of the Radical Hospitality of your children.

Where to Go From Here?

Share the teaching materials in this chapter that are designed for a Sunday school lesson, children's worship lesson, or special teaching session. There are teaching materials for separate use with preschool, elementary, and older elementary (tween) children. Decide as a group how and when you will teach this material to the children. Set a date for the teaching of these lessons. After the lessons are taught, determine how you will use the ideas for Radical Hospitality that the children have chosen. You might designate a preschool teacher who will share the ideas of the younger children, but you will want to invite representative elementary and older children to share the ideas of their age groups.

Celebrate and Affirm the Ideas of Children

Hold a pizza party or ice cream social and invite children to share their ideas for Radical Hospitality as a result of their lessons and activities. Let the children decide ways they will communicate their ideas with the congregation. Encourage the children to practice Radical Hospitality in the life of the church and in their schools and communities, but focus on one or more ideas for Radical Hospitality that the children can do together at church.

Discuss ways the children can enlist the help of the congregation. Children can be encouraged to present ideas at your church's administrative board or in a worship time.

Give the children helpful advice on how to get started on a mission project involving Radical Hospitality that the children have selected. Children can make posters, write articles for the newsletter, and share with Sunday school classes. Help the children develop the steps they will take to ensure that the mission project is well received by the congregation. Guide them in the necessary steps to carry out the mission project.

An Example of Radical Hospitality:

Your children have chosen to host a Christmas party for needy children who attend an inner-city church in your city.

1. Gain the support of your pastor, staff, and church leaders.
2. Have one child or several children speak in your worship service about this vision of the children.
3. Have one child or several children write newsletter articles.
4. Have children make posters.
5. Have children speak with Sunday school classes and other groups in the church to secure Christmas gifts for each child.
6. Talk with the pastor of the inner-city church to secure names of children and their Christmas wish lists.
7. Plan refreshments, games, and decorations for the event.
8. Have children shop for gifts and wrap presents.
9. Enlist the help of adults to make treats.
10. Invite the children.
11. Decorate the church.
12. Host the party.
13. Have a time for the children to share their experiences and let them decide if they wish to make this a yearly mission outreach project of your church.

A Child Practices Radical Hospitality

Objective:

The children will:
- Hear John 6:1-14.
- Learn about a child in Bible times who practiced Radical Hospitality.
- Learn ways they can practice Radical Hospitality today.

Bible Story:

John 6:1-14: A child shares his lunch with Jesus. Jesus blesses the food and feeds many hungry people.

Bible Verse:

A youth here has five barley loaves and two fish.
John 6:9

Focus for the Teacher

Jesus' feeding of the five thousand is recorded in all four of our Gospels, but it is only in John's Gospel that we learn that Jesus is able to perform his miraculous feeding because of the Radical Hospitality of a child (John 6:1-14)! Imagine the mother of this child preparing his lunch for the day, anticipating that the young boy would become hungry as the day wore on. Our text does not tell us if Andrew asked permission of the lad to take the five loaves and two fish, but we cannot imagine Andrew simply snatching the boy's lunch away without asking! Our Scripture informs us that Andrew had observed that the only available food in the large crowd belonged to a young boy, and this supply was certainly not enough to feed the entire gathering. No doubt, there were others in the crowd who had a food supply, but they were either hiding it or refusing to give it up. The text leads us to believe that the young boy readily gave his lunch to Andrew. Did the young boy have second thoughts? Was he afraid his mother would be angry with him for giving his carefully prepared lunch away? Was the boy really hungry and looking forward to the delicious meal in his basket? We do not know, but somewhere along the way the child pushed aside thoughts of hunger and worry to present his offering to Jesus. Whether he realized it or not, this boy practiced Radical Hospitality.

The Gospel of Matthew presents us with an interesting insight. Matthew adds an intriguing phrase at the end of his story recorded in Matthew 14:13-21. He says, "About five thousand men plus women and children had eaten." Matthew is simply telling us an amazing fact when he uses the words "plus women and children." He is letting us know that the women and children did not get counted! An uncounted boy was responsible for the gift of Radical Hospitality, a pivotal action that is the turning point in our story. Doubting Andrew is not sure the gift of the boy will be sufficient, saying, "A youth here has five barley loaves and two fish. But what good is that for a crowd like this?" (John 6:9). Yet Jesus confirms that the boy's offering is more than sufficient as he commands the people to sit down.

Do we believe that the gifts of our children are sufficient? Unfortunately, some congregations place children among the uncounted when it comes to taking their gifts seriously. Congregations that encourage children to practice Radical Hospitality will honor and value the gifts of children rather than cast them aside as insufficient, viewing children as among the uncounted in the church.

What a story this lad had to share with his family when he returned home! Yet, one is left to wonder if the story of the Radical Hospitality of this boy impacted the crowd at all. Were they so caught up in the miracle of having their stomachs filled and their hunger satisfied that they failed to grasp the Radical Hospitality of a child whose name we will never know and the Radical Hospi-

tality of a man named Jesus? This child, through his willingness to share, represented for the people and for us a radical sign of the kingdom of God at work. God can take our gifts of Radical Hospitality, bless them, and multiply them, no matter how small or insignificant they may seem to us.

God can take our gifts of Radical Hospitality, bless them, and multiply them, no matter how small or insignificant they may seem to us.

Like the act of Radical Hospitality of this child in John's Gospel, the radical acts of hospitality shared by children in our churches often go unnoticed. Yet, congregations that make children a priority will not only praise and affirm the radical acts of hospitality by children, but they will also work to teach children what Radical Hospitality means and how they can be involved in carrying out deeds that are radical and life-changing. Surely the lad in John's Gospel was taught Radical Hospitality from his Jewish tradition. The Jewish people knew that in their past, they had been foreigners and aliens in a strange land, so they were committed to reaching out with Radical Hospitality to strangers.

This child in our Bible story can provide a powerful example to our children today of Radical Hospitality that made a difference in the ministry of Jesus and in a large crowd of people. They can, then, be inspired to seek out ways to practice Radical Hospitality themselves, both in the life of their congregation and in their schools and communities.

Radical Hospitality

Welcome the Children With Hospitality

Welcome each child by name. Put a sticker of a smiley face on each child's hand or clothing. Let the child know you are glad he or she is present. Have the children color a picture of the Bible story (page 20). As they color, talk to the children about the picture. Ask them to tell you what they think the child is doing. Have the children guess which figure represents Jesus.

Share the Bible Story (John 6:1-14)

Gather the children and have them sit on a rug. Read the children the story of the boy who gave his lunch to Jesus, using a preschool Bible or a children's storybook. Show the children a picture of the story, pointing out to them Jesus, Andrew, and the young boy.

Reinforce the Story

Teach the children motions to use when you read the story to them. When they hear the name "Jesus" they are to wave their hands above their heads. When they hear the name "Andrew" they are to stomp their feet, and when they hear "young boy" they are to clap their hands.

Jesus *(wave hands above head)* sees a large group of people. He wants to teach them. The people stay with Jesus *(wave hands above head)* all day. The people get very hungry. Andrew *(stomp feet)*, one of Jesus' *(wave hands above head)* helpers, goes to see if any of the people have food to eat. He finds a young boy *(clap hands)* who brought a lunch with him. The young boy *(clap hands)* has five pieces of bread and two pieces of fish. He gives his lunch to Andrew *(stomp feet)*. When Jesus *(wave hands above head)* sees what the young boy *(clap hands)* gives, he says a prayer and feeds all of the hungry people! The young boy *(clap hands)* is so glad to help Jesus *(wave hands above head)*.

Prepare

Photocopy the picture of Jesus and the boy (page 20) for each child.

Provide smiley-face stickers and crayons.

Prepare

Provide a preschool Bible or children's storybook.

Play a Bible Game

Play a version of the popular children's game "Duck, Duck, Goose." Select a child to be the leader. Tell the child to say "Andrew, Andrew" instead of "duck, duck" and to say "Jesus" instead of "goose" as he or she goes around the circle tapping children on the shoulder. When a child who is tapped hears the name "Jesus," he or she runs around the circle and returns to his or her place. If this child returns before the leader catches him or her, the child is safe. If not, the child becomes the one doing the tapping and chasing, and the leader takes the spot of the child who was being chased.

Practicing Radical Hospitality in Learning Centers

Prepare

Set up several learning centers.

Set up several learning centers for preschool children. Among these should be a home center, a block center, a picture book center, a "dress-up" center, and a music center. You may already have your preschool classroom arranged with centers. Send the children to whichever center they wish to go. Tell the children that you are going to visit each center and suggest to the children ways they can share with other children. Watch as the children play. After a while, suggest that one child share his or her toy with another child or let the child play with that toy. Offer other suggestions on ways all children can be included. Adults and older children would not consider this Radical Hospitality, but the preschool child is very centered on self. By encouraging the children to take turns and share, you are offering them valuable lessons in extending Radical Hospitality to others in their class.

Radical Hospitality During Snack Time

Prepare

Provide a simple snack. Be aware of any allergies.

Have the children serve one another during snack time. Let one child at a time come forward and receive a snack item. Have that child take the snack item to another child. Keep doing this until all the children have served one another. Remind the children that Jesus wants us to share with others. If there is a visitor in the class, let the children serve the visitor first.

Hospitality Tea Party

Help the children practice Radical Hospitality by planning a tea party in which they will invite another Sunday school class to join them for snacks. Talk about ways you might decorate your room to welcome the friends to your tea party. During the following Sunday school sessions, take some time to make invitations for the children to deliver to the Sunday school class and to make decorations to hang around the room. Assist the children in making snacks. Let the children serve their friends when they arrive for the tea party.

Invitations: Give each child a copy of the invitation (page 21) and a piece of construction paper. Show the children how to fold the construction paper in half like a card. Then show the children how to open the card and glue the invitation to the inside. Let the children decorate the cover of the cards with crayons or markers and stickers. Deliver the cards to the Sunday school class you are inviting to the tea party.

Decorations: Cover the table with a piece of mural paper or a plastic tablecloth. Let the children decorate the paper or tablecloth with crayons and stickers. Provide crepe paper streamers. Let the children help you decide how to display the streamers in the room.

Cookies: Use your favorite cookie recipe or the recipe printed below.

The Boy's Lunch Pudding Cups

35 vanilla wafers
2 cups cold milk
1 pkg. vanilla-flavored instant pudding
1½ cups thawed nondairy whipped topping
gummy fish

Place the vanilla wafers in a resealable plastic bag. Let the children take turns crushing the wafers. Set the crushed wafers aside.

Pour milk into a large bowl and add the pudding mix. Let the children take turns stirring the mixture until it is well blended. Let stand five minutes.

Stir in the whipped topping. Gradually stir in one cup of crushed wafers. Spoon into paper or plastic cups. Top with remaining crushed wafers and refrigerate. Just before serving, decorate each top with two gummy fish.

Closing Prayer

Thank you, God, for our Bible story of a young boy who shared with others. Help me to share with others. Amen.

Prepare

Photocopy the invitation (page 21) for each child.

Provide construction paper, glue, crayons or markers, stickers, mural paper or a plastic tablecloth, crepe paper streamers, and tape.

Provide ingredients and utensils for making cookies.

Radical Hospitality

Ask the children to bring their lunch boxes to church for a special lesson. Have extra lunch boxes available.

Prepare

Provide extra lunch boxes.

Welcome the Children With Hospitality

Welcome each child by name. Have them make cards for members of your congregation who have limited ability to leave home. Instruct the children to fold pieces of construction paper in half. Let each child decorate the front of the card with his or her drawing. Help the child write a short message of hospitality inside the card. Mail the cards.

Prepare

Provide construction paper and markers or crayons.

Share the Bible Story (John 6:1-14)

Gather the children and have them sit on a rug. Have a storyteller tell the children Andrew's story (see page 21).

Prepare

Photocopy the script (page 21).

Recruit an adult to portray Andrew and provide a simple Bible-times costume.

Play a Bible Fishing Game

Construct a fishing pond. Use a large piece of cardboard that is tall enough so the children cannot see on the other side. Make a fishing rod from a dowel rod, yarn, and a clothespin.

Have your assistant sit in a chair on the back side of the fishing pond. Ask a question from the list below and let children take turns fishing.

When a child throws the fishing line over the top of the cardboard fishing pond, your assistant will attach the correct answer to the clothespin. Remind the children that Andrew was a fisherman when he met Jesus. Let everyone have a turn at fishing, even if you repeat questions.

Prepare

Construct a fishing pond and a fishing rod. You will need a large piece of cardboard, a dowel rod, yarn, a clothespin, and scissors.

Photocopy and cut apart the answers to the questions (page 22).

1. Why was Jesus with the large crowd? (*He was teaching about God.*)
2. Why were the people sad and upset that day? (*It was late in the day and the people were hungry.*)
3. Which disciple of Jesus went into the crowd to look for food? (*Andrew*)

4. Who gave his lunch to Jesus? *(a boy)*
5. What food did the boy bring for lunch? *(two fish and five loaves of bread)*
6. How many men were present? *(5,000)*
7. What did Jesus do with the boy's lunch? *(He blessed the food and used it to feed the people.)*
8. How many baskets of food were left over? *(twelve)*
9. What was the name of Andrew's brother? *(Peter)*
10. What other disciple is mentioned in our story? *(Philip)*

Teach the Children About Radical Hospitality

Write the words *radical* and *hospitality* on the board. Tell the children that the boy helped Jesus by giving his lunch to him. Explain that he did something that we in the church call *Radical Hospitality*. Let the children say both words several times. Tell the children that the word *radical* means something very different, something out of the ordinary. *Hospitality* is sharing with others in such a way that they know they are loved and cared for by others. Radical Hospitality=great love, care, and kindness. Think of an example of Radical Hospitality in your congregation that the children might relate to and be familiar with and share this with the children. Say to the children, "The boy who brought his lunch to Jesus showed great love, caring, and kindness to Jesus and to the crowd of people. Maybe he was hungry himself and wanted to eat his lunch, but he gave it to Jesus and many people were fed."

Practice Radical Hospitality

Give each child two fish cut-outs and five loaves of bread cut-outs. Have the children place their fish and bread in their lunch boxes.

Have a person visit your class dressed as Jesus and another person visit your class dressed as Andrew. Tell the children that they are to pretend to be the boy who gave his lunch to Jesus. They will want to say "yes" when Andrew asks them a question.

Have Andrew stop in front of a child and ask if she or he would be willing to give her or his lunch to Jesus. When the child says yes, Andrew will take the child's lunch box to Jesus. Jesus will hold up the lunch box and say to the child, "Thank you for showing Radical Hospitality. Thank you for showing great love, caring, and kindness." Andrew will then take the lunch box back to the child and select another child until each child has had the opportunity to respond.

Prepare

Provide chalkboard and chalk, markerboard and markers, or newsprint and markers.

Prepare

Photocopy and cut out the bread and the fish (page 20) so that each child has two fish and five loaves of bread.

Recruit an adult to portray Jesus and an adult to portray Andrew. Provide Bible-times costumes.

Practice Radical Hospitality in the Church

If possible, take the children into your sanctuary. Select a child in the class who will pretend to be a new visitor to your church. Place the other children in pews or chairs as if they are gathered for your church's worship service. Have the visitor enter the sanctuary. Teach the children how to practice Radical Hospitality to this stranger. Have one child get up and say "hello" to the child, telling the child his or her name. Have one child get up and get the visitor a children's worship bag if you have those in your church. Ask one child to tell the visitor what will happen during the children's sermon if your church has this time for children in your worship service. Have one child tell the visitor about children's worship and volunteer to go with the visitor to children's worship if your church has this time for children. Have the children roleplay their parts several times with different children taking various roles. Eventually, have one child practice all of the roles at one time with a pretend visitor. Repeat this process until all the children have a turn. Encourage children to watch for children who visit the church and be willing to go and speak to them and welcome them. Remind the children to gain their parents' permission to welcome a child visitor.

Practice Radical Hospitality in the World

Have the children think of ways they can practice Radical Hospitality. Some of these ideas will take the efforts of the entire congregation. Have the children select the ideas they like best and share these with your children's ministry committee.

Serve Fish Crackers for a Snack

As you bless the food, remind the children that Jesus blessed the food that a young boy brought to him.

Closing Prayer

Thank you, God, for our Sunday school lesson today about a boy who shared his lunch. Thank you for our church and all the ways we reach out to others in need and help them. God, help us to show love and kindness to others. In Jesus' name. Amen.

Prepare

Provide fish crackers, juice, napkins, and cups. Be aware of any allergies.

Tween
(Older Elementary)

Radical Hospitality

Welcome the Children With Hospitality

Welcome the children by name. Instruct them to go to the hospitality box in your room. Have each child open the box, reach in, and select a slip of paper. This paper will have the name of someone in your congregation who is currently serving in the military. Provide note paper so the child can write a note of appreciation to that military person. Mail the notes.

Bible Study (John 6:1-14)

Have tweens take turns reading aloud the Bible story from John 6:1-14. Have the tweens acts out the skit entitled "Fishy Hospitality" (page 23).

Report the Story

Divide your tweens into groups, depending on the size of your class. You may choose to have the tweens work on one or more activity depending on how many groups you are able to form.

Group One: Work together to write the story as a newspaper account. Describe the sensational events of the feeding of the five thousand. Interview the young boy and get his reaction.

Group Two: Work together to create a cartoon or poster drawing of what happened when the boy returned home and told his family about his experience. Explain to the tweens that we are not certain if any of the boy's family members were present at the feeding of the five thousand, but tell the tweens they are to pretend the family of the boy was at home.

Group Three: Work together as television reporters and write out an interview with Andrew about what happened in our Bible story. Let

Prepare

Decorate a box.

Write the names of persons in your congregation who are in the military on slips of paper. Place the names in the box.

Provide note paper and pens or pencils.

Prepare

Photocopy the skit "Fishy Hospitality" (page 23) for each tween.

Optional: Provide Bible-times costumes.

Prepare

Provide paper and pencils.

one person be the television interviewer and another play the role of Andrew. Have the interviewer ask Andrew questions concerning the incident of the feeding of the five thousand people.

Bring the groups back together and have each of them share.

Understanding Radical Hospitality

Prepare

Provide dictionaries along with chalkboard and chalk, markerboard and markers, or newsprint and markers.

Give class members dictionaries and have them work in pairs. Have one person look up the word *radical* and another the word *hospitality*. On the board, list all of the meanings of *radical* and all of the meanings of *hospitality* that the children find. Talk about why this young boy practiced Radical Hospitality, rather than simply hospitality.

Have the class list ways they practice hospitality at church, at school, and in their community. Then ask them to think of ways to practice Radical Hospitality. Help the children understand the difference between hospitality and Radical Hospitality. For example, hospitality is greeting someone the children know at church by saying hello. Radical Hospitality is welcoming a complete stranger, perhaps a new child who has come to visit the church.

Putting Radical Hospitality Into Practice

Ask the tweens to brainstorm about several ways children in the church could practice and lead the church in extending Radical Hospitality. Several ideas are listed below, but encourage your tweens to come up with their own ideas. Tell them that their ideas will be shared with the children's ministry team and church leaders. Ask them to select the ideas that the group likes best.

Ways Tweens Can Practice Radical Hospitality

1. Rather than receiving gifts for his or her birthday party, the tween holds a mission birthday party and designates money or items for a selected mission.
2. Tweens reach out to elderly neighbors and volunteer to help with yard work, walking the dog, or other chores.
3. Tweens agree to look around the sanctuary on Sunday morning. When they see new child visitors at the church, they will welcome those children and inform them about the children's program at church. Tweens will introduce the children to other children in the church and give them information about what

is going to happen in worship that involves children. (Children will need training so that this act of Radical Hospitality can be carried out in an effective and capable manner. Sunday school teachers, your pastor, or your children's ministry team can offer a training time for the tweens in your church.)

4. Tweens volunteer at the local Humane Society or another agency in the community.
5. The class or several tween friends get together to plan and host a Christmas party for underprivileged children in the community.
6. Tweens serve meals at a homeless shelter, along with parents.
7. Tweens write letters to soldiers and collect supplies and phone calling cards for the soldiers.
8. Tweens invite children from a congregation of an ethnicity other than their own to join them for a skating or bowling party.
9. Tweens volunteer to read books to children who are ill.
10. Tweens mentor younger children in the church by befriending them, sitting with them in church, and affirming them.

A Radical Hospitality Covenant

This is a prayerful commitment on the part of older elementary children as they discern one way to practice Radical Hospitality in their church, school, or community.

Tell the tweens not to sign the covenant until they have prayed about what they would like to do and not until they have discussed the idea with their parents. Tweens might do this as individuals or secure the help of other friends. Family members will want to be involved, offering support, but letting the older elementary child take the lead.

Provide a copy of the covenant for each tween in your class. Have extra copies for visitors who may wish to participate.

Closing Prayer

Thank you, God, for our Bible story today about a boy who practiced Radical Hospitality by sharing his lunch with others. Help me to reach out to others at school, in my community, and wherever I go to share the love of Christ. Show me ways to practice Radical Hospitality this week. In Jesus' name. Amen.

Prepare

Photocopy the "Radical Hospitality Covenant" (page 24) for each tween.

Families Can Teach Children Radical Hospitality

Parents are the primary teachers of faith formation for their children. Certainly the church must partner with parents in this important endeavor; however, parents must take seriously their role. Families can teach and demonstrate Radical Hospitality in the ways they relate to others. Families can practice Radical Hospitality in the ordinary events of everyday living. How do children see parents treating others in their neighborhood? Do family members go out of their way to welcome newcomers to the neighborhood, perhaps inviting them for a meal or preparing a special dish of food for them?

How do children observe parents treating their schoolteachers, and what actions do parents take to encourage their children to be sensitive to the needs of other classmates? Do parents go out of their way to encourage all children on the child's sporting team, even offering words of affirmation for children on the opposing team?

Children can learn valuable lessons about Radical Hospitality from watching their parents and siblings, but families should covenant together to share experiences of Radical Hospitality.

Suggestions for Ways Families Can Practice Radical Hospitality

1. Invite an older adult in the neighborhood whose spouse is no longer living to share a meal with your family, especially during the holidays.
2. Help single parents in your neighborhood by having older children in the family watch the children while a single parent enjoys a "night out."
3. Suggest to the child's coach that they welcome the opposing team at a sporting competition and offer them assistance and hospitality.
4. Serve a meal together at a homeless shelter.
5. Volunteer together at a mission or animal shelter.
6. Be aware of neighbors who have had surgery and offer to walk their pets for them while they recuperate.
7. Show appreciation at holidays to the custodian at your child's school. This is a person who is often forgotten and unappreciated. Have children make cards for him or her.
8. Say a prayer at mealtime for the person in your neighborhood who is the most annoying neighbor or the grouchiest neighbor. Help children understand that we do not always know what other persons face in life. That particular neighbor may have problems, disappointments, or hurts or have a past history of difficulties.
9. Encourage your child to have a birthday party in which he or she does not receive gifts, but rather each child invited to the party brings money or items for a designated mission.
10. Set up a lemonade stand in the neighborhood that offers "free lemonade" and have your children pass out lemonade to neighbors.

Stories of Children
Practicing Radical Hospitality

The confirmation class of Christ United Methodist, in Franklin, Tennessee, share a Saturday evening with the worshipers at Sixty-First United Methodist Church, an inner-city church in Nashville, Tennessee. They prepare and serve a meal along with their confirmation mentors and then attend worship.

Children at State Street United Methodist, Bowling Green, Kentucky, enjoyed their annual Advent Fair where they made Advent crafts. During this event they also collected toys and food items for needy families and gave their collections to the Salvation Army for distribution. However, the children realized that they could practice Radical Hospitality if they were to deliver the gifts and food items themselves. Now, rather than spending all of their time at the Advent Fair making crafts, they spend the majority of the time on acts of Radical Hospitality. Prior to the Advent Fair, they have been assigned a needy family in the community for whom they buy presents and food items. At the Advent Fair, families and children wrap the presents and then deliver the presents and food items to the needy families. Being able to meet the families has made a far greater impact on the children than just collecting the items and giving them to an organization for distribution.

Christ United Methodist, Franklin, Tennessee, prepares meals for homeless men every Thursday evening during the winter months through the Room in the Inn program of the Nashville community. The children of the church always enjoyed making placemats for the men and putting together health kits. Eventually the children determined that making placemats for the men was an expression of hospitality, but not an act of Radical Hospi-

tality. The children decided that they wanted to meet the men and serve the meal. Usually the men had no food choices; they simply ate what they were served. The children created a menu, offering the men a choice between several meats and vegetables. The children decorated the room, served the meal, sat and talked with the men, and sang for them. The parents of the children prepared the food and helped with cleanup. This was a great blessing for these homeless men, who rarely were able to be in contact with children and who greatly enjoyed their conversation.

The confirmation class of Brentwood United Methodist, Brentwood, Tennessee, attends the Special Olympics basketball tournament hosted by Belmont University in Nashville, Tennessee. They sit in the stands and cheer the participants, then interact with the athletes after the event. Several members of the confirmation class also volunteer at Harvest Hands, a community-development program sponsored by the church that reaches out to underprivileged families in the South Nashville area. The confirmation students, along with their mentors ("Friends in Faith"), engage in after-school tutoring.

Amelia and her family attend Broomfield United Methodist, Broomfield, Colorado. Recently a family from New Zealand moved into her neighborhood. Amelia promptly invited the children in the new family to attend church. To date, Amelia has invited most of her classmates to join her at Wacky Wednesday, a Christian-based after-school enrichment opportunity at her church. She can be credited with increasing the number of those who now attend on a regular basis by more than half a dozen of her classmates.

Art: Robert S. Jones
© 2001 Cokesbury

Art: Megan Jeffery
© 2000 Abingdon Press

You are invited to a

Tea Party

Date: _____

Time: _____

Place: _____

Script for Andrew
by Daphna Flegal

I'm Andrew. I am a friend of Jesus. In fact, I introduced my brother, Peter, to Jesus. Peter and I, along with some other friends, go with him as he travels around the countryside teaching people about God. Many, many people come to see Jesus wherever he goes. Some people want Jesus to heal them. Some people want Jesus to bless them. Other people want to hear Jesus teach them about God.

Once Jesus was teaching a crowd of people. There were five thousand men. And there were women and children not counted in the five thousand. They stayed all day long. When Jesus finished teaching, it was late. The people started getting upset. They were tired and hungry.

Jesus turned to Philip, one of our friends, and asked, "Where will we buy food to feed all these people?"

"It would take a lot of money to buy food for all these people," answered Philip.

As I was looking at all the people who needed to be fed, I spotted a boy holding his lunch. He had five loaves of bread and two fish. The boy looked at his lunch. He looked at me. Then he held out his lunch to me.

I didn't see how five loaves of bread and two fish were going to help very much, but I took the boy and his lunch to Jesus.

Jesus had everyone sit down on the grass. He blessed the bread and fish. Then he started passing food to the people. Everyone had plenty to eat. There were even twelve baskets of leftovers! All because one boy shared five loaves of bread and two fish, more than five thousand people were fed.

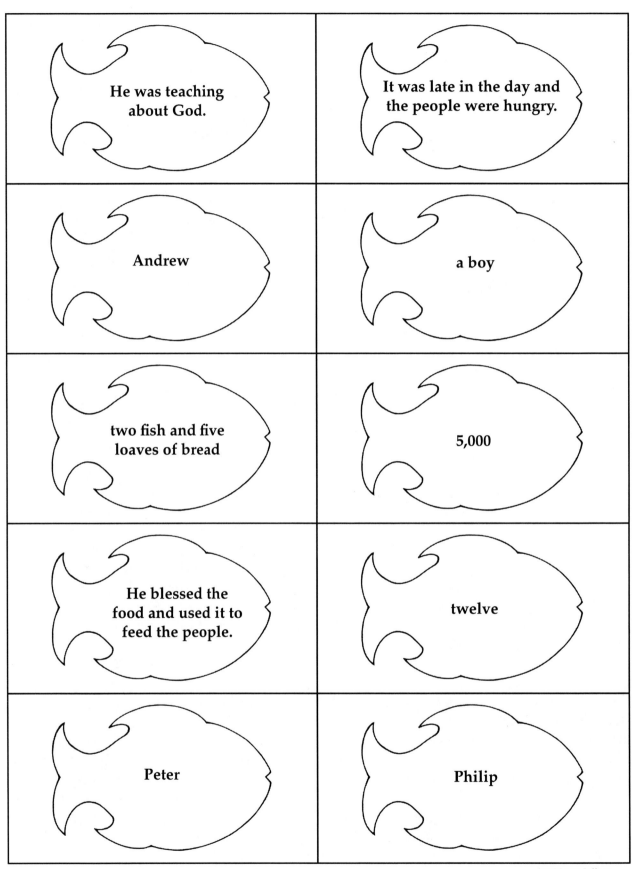

He was teaching about God.

It was late in the day and the people were hungry.

Andrew

a boy

two fish and five loaves of bread

5,000

He blessed the food and used it to feed the people.

twelve

Peter

Philip

Fishy Hospitality
by Rita Hays

(Characters: Mother, Adam, Jesus, Philip, Andrew, Disciples, Crowd.)

Mother *(handing Adam a lunch box)*: Adam, I have packed a nice lunch for you, five loaves of barley bread and two fish. I know that is one of your favorite meals. Go on and let me know what Jesus teaches about!

Adam: Thanks, Mom. I will come home and tell you everything Jesus does and says!

Jesus *(to Philip)*: The crowd is very large today. They look hungry. Where are we going to get enough food to feed all of these people?

Philip: My paycheck for six months would not be enough money to feed all of these people!

Andrew: Jesus, I spotted a young boy in the crowd. He has a lunch his mother prepared for him. In his lunch box he has five barley loaves and two fish. Of course, that little food will not even begin to feed this large, hungry crowd. At least his mother was smart enough to pack him a lunch.

Jesus: Tell all the people to sit down. Andrew, go and ask the boy if he is willing to share his lunch with us.

Andrew *(to Adam)*: Young man, the people here are very hungry, but we do not have any food. We noticed you were getting ready to take a bite out of your lunch. Before you take that first bite, please listen to me. Jesus wants to know if you would be willing to share your lunch with others.

Adam: If Jesus needs my lunch, I am glad to share. My parents taught me that it is good and right to share with others in need.

(Jesus takes bread, blesses it, and hands some to the disciples. The disciples give food to the crowd.)

Jesus *(to disciples)*: If everyone is full, go and gather up the leftovers.

Disciples: Jesus, there are twelve baskets of leftovers!

Crowd: This man Jesus is a great prophet!

(Adam runs home very excited.)

Adam: Mom, guess what happened!

Mother: Tell me. I want to know everything that happened and everything Jesus said.

Adam: Jesus talked for a long time. I was getting very hungry. Just about the time I was getting ready to eat my bread and fish, over comes one of Jesus' disciples. He asked me if I would give my food to feed the hungry people.

Mother: What did you say?

Adam*:* I said, "Yes!" You and Dad have taught me to share with those in need and I thought this was the right thing to do.

Mother: Yes, son, you did the right thing! But tell me what happened after you gave your food to Jesus.

Adam: Jesus took the food, blessed it, and fed all of the people. We were so full we could not eat another bite. And to top it off, there were twelve baskets of leftovers.

Mother: Jesus is a great man and prophet.

Adam: I'll second that!

Radical Hospitality Covenant

I, _____,

after praying to God and talking with my

family, will practice Radical Hospitality by

_____

_____

_____.

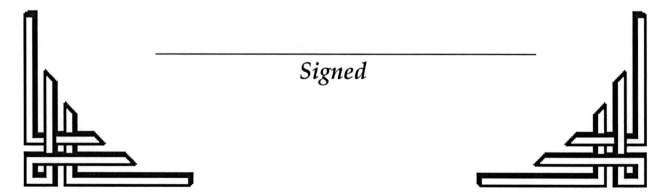

_____
Signed

2.

Passionate Worship for Children

Introduction

First-grader Maggie Shannon worships God with both child-like humility and passionate devotion. During the worship service, her senses come alive as she participates in praising God. When the congregation bows their heads for prayer, Maggie bows her head. When the pastor speaks with the children during the special time set aside for them, Maggie listens attentively. When the choir sings, Maggie sways to the music, moving her hands in imitation of the choir director. Maggie honors God with her worship because she praises God with uninhibited enthusiasm and joy.

Maggie belongs to a congregation that values the important place of children in the worshiping community. Her congregation recognizes that children imitate others as they worship, so they accept their role as teachers who model faith for a new generation. Maggie worships in a congregation that demonstrates understanding when children become restless in worship and squirm in their seats, yet also affirms children when they praise God in their own unique ways. Maggie joyfully embraces worship because her community of faith joyfully embraces children and offers them the gift of belonging and participating in worship.

Fifth-grader Juan Garcia encounters Christ through the sacrament of Holy Communion. He listens carefully to the liturgy as the familiar phrases wash over him and resonate in his heart and mind. The words convey a message of grace, love, and acceptance to him. His favorite part of worship comes when he and his family make their way to the altar and humbly bow on bended knees to receive the bread and juice. Juan takes seriously this time in worship, for this is a time of true happiness for him. The invitation assures him that he is welcome to come and partake in this special meal that remembers Jesus. He eagerly stretches out his palms as the pastor breaks off a piece of bread and places it in his cupped hands. Juan listens as the pastor talks directly to him, saying, "Juan, the body of Christ broken for you." Juan takes time to pray to God, thanking him for Jesus and his love for him. Juan carefully dips the bread into the cup as the pastor addresses him again with the words, "Juan, this is the blood of Christ shed for you." Whenever he participates in Holy Communion, Juan remembers God loves him. Juan experiences a holy, passionate moment in worship.

Juan worships in a community of faith that welcomes children to participate in Holy Communion. His church recognizes that children may not fully understand the liturgy or the ritual, yet the congregation senses that the presence of children enriches this family meal. Like Juan, other children need the affirmation of their congregations to participate in Holy Communion as welcomed children. They also need churches that value the importance of sensory experiences for children in worship such as Juan discovers in Holy Communion through touching the bread, dipping in the cup, and kneeling at the altar.

Children arrive for worship as spiritual beings. Worship comes alive for them when they are able to use their senses in worship. Touch, smell, sound, and movement capture children in worship and draw them into the service. Children like Maggie and Juan engage in Passionate Worship because their church mentors find ways to help these children use their God-given senses. Also, church members model for them devoted and fervent worship practices that spring from their own joy in worshiping God. In addition, pastors, Sunday teachers, parents, and church leaders devote themselves to teaching children about Passionate Worship. These congregations not only invest time in teaching children about Passionate Worship, but they also plan quality worship. Worship services reflect the needs not only of adults and youth, but of children as well. Congregations value and bless children when they guide them toward ways to express Passionate Worship. They never seek to stifle the variety of ways children worship God, but welcome the anointing work of the Holy Spirit in the lives of children, which draws them to worship God passionately.

What is Passionate Worship?
What does it have to do with children?

Passionate Worship flows from our belief that God created us to worship and longs to hear our heartfelt offerings of praise. Through Passionate Worship we connect with God, and God connects with us. We open ourselves up to hear God speaking to us, guiding us, instructing us, and leading us to deeper paths of commitment and service. We encounter God, God encounters us, and our lives are changed forever!

Passionate Worship deepens our relationship with God and Jesus Christ. Passionate Worship offers hope and healing to shattered lives, brings clarity to our uncertainties about God's call, and guides our direction, outlook, and motivation as we struggle with daily life decisions. Passionate Worship draws us into a loving relationship with others and offers us a new perspective to view our world.

Congregations that endeavor to offer worship experiences that present opportunities for Passionate Worship begin by opening themselves up to the Spirit of God. As leaders gather with the intention of planning worship services that enrich worship for all persons, they call upon the Holy Spirit to lead and guide them. They take their worship-planning tasks seriously, but they also trust that God's Holy Spirit becomes the agent to work in the hearts and lives of those who worship. Passionate Worship begins with the recognition of the work of the Holy Spirit both in worship and in worship planning. With ultimate trust in the workings of the Holy Spirit, worship leaders give careful attention to all elements of the worship service.

Passionate Worship does not depend upon a particular style of worship; rather, it evolves from passionate leaders who do all in their power to see that each worship service allows persons to praise God without the distraction of poorly planned music, incessant announcements, presentation-software glitches, untrained acolytes, ill-prepared sermons, error-filled bulletins, and unprepared worship participants.

Unfortunately, some of the poorest planning in worship takes place where children are concerned. Often, churches ignore the needs of children when planning worship. Yet, children need and want worship experiences that allow them to encounter God in a vital, life-changing relationship.

When planning worship, leaders should examine the aspects of the worship service that pertain to children. Choose adults and youth for children's sermons who relate well to children. Carefully train these individuals in the choice of vocabulary words and the limited attention span of children. Have two sets of children's worship bags, one filled with coloring and reading materials relevant for younger children and another for older children. Train acolytes and children who are worship participants. Plan quality children's church time with sound theological curriculum for children. Encourage pastors to address children occasionally in sermons. Invite children to participate in Holy Communion.

What kind of attitude does your congregation have toward children in the worshiping community? Do congregants allow for the interruptions of children or do they view children as a distraction to their own ability to worship? Educating congregations about children in worship gives worshipers a more realistic picture of expectations from children and a greater empathy toward parents who are trying to quiet a restless child.

Passionate Worship transforms the lives of children. Children discover a God who loves them, who cares about their concerns, and who seeks to be in relationship with them. Passionate Worship heals the lives of children. Children enter our sanctuaries with their own hurts, problems, and challenges. In Passionate Worship, they meet a God who deeply cares for them. They learn of a Christ who blesses them as he blessed children in his own ministry. They pray to a compassionate God, trusting that God hears their prayers, acknowledges their problems, and walks beside them on their faith journey. Passionate Worship guides children in their future decisions. Passionate Worship helps children grow in their Christian faith. Passionate Worship introduces children to Jesus Christ and invites children into a lifetime of service to others.

Passionate Worship draws the people of God together in loving relationship with one another. Children belong to the community of faith as blessed gifts from God. Passionate Worship for children begins and ends with a community of faith that models and teaches them what it means and what it looks like to worship God passionately. Yet, children teach and model for the community as well. The ability and gift to worship God passionately belongs to all of God's children, regardless of age.

Passionate Worship transforms the lives of children.

Workshop for Lesson Two

Encourage the members of your children's ministry team, your Sunday school teachers, and other volunteers in your children's ministry area to gather for a time of teaching and reflection on the ways children in the church may be involved in Passionate Worship.

Prayer and Welcome

Reflections on Matthew 21:12-16

Divide your group into two teams. Select one person in each team as the recorder. Have the two teams discuss and then come back as one group to share their insights.

Team One: Jesus Group

• Write down all of the arguments Jesus gave in the Scriptures or might have given for why the children should be allowed to worship.

• Write down all of the arguments why children should be allowed to worship Jesus in your church.

Team Two: Chief Priests

• Write down all of the arguments the religious leaders gave or might have given for why the children should not be allowed to worship in the Temple area.

• Write down arguments why persons might feel that children should not be allowed to worship Jesus in your sanctuary.

Affirm the Ways Your Children Now Engage in Passionate Worship

Divide the group into pairs. Go into your sanctuary. Ask each partner pair to find a place in the sanctuary where they believe that the children practice Passionate Worship or where events occur that help children to practice Passionate Worship. Have them stand or sit in this area.

Ideas:
1. Near Communion table
2. In choir loft (children's choir)
3. By candles
4. In pews
5. Area where children gather for children's sermon
6. Baptismal font
7. Area where children's worship bags are kept
8. Choir or piano
9. Pulpit area
10. Place where Bible is kept
11. Altar area
12. Area where children's worship takes place (This takes place outside the sanctuary area, but may be mentioned as a reminder of the importance of children's church.)
13. Area where video display equipment is housed

Discuss ways children in your sanctuary and congregation are hindered from practicing Passionate Worship. Discuss ways you can remedy each situation. Write a prayer of confession to the children asking them and God for forgiveness.

Where to Go From Here?

Share the teaching materials in this chapter that are designed for a Sunday school lesson, children's worship lesson, or special teaching session. There are teaching materials for separate use with preschool, elementary, and older elementary (tween) children. Decide as a group how and when you will teach this material to the children. Set a date for the teaching of these lessons. After the lessons are taught, determine how you will use the ideas for Passionate Worship that the children have chosen. Invite your pastor and worship leaders to be present when the ideas are shared.

Celebrate and Affirm the Ideas of Children

Invite the children for a special day of celebration with the pastors and worship leaders in your church. Ask your pastor and worship leaders to design a worship service that is kid-friendly and will help children engage in Passionate Worship. Members of the children's ministry team will need to provide ideas such as a puppet show, catchy praise songs, dancing to Christian music, and Holy Communion where the children are allowed to bring in the Communion cloth and elements. Have this service prepared ahead of time. Gather in an area outside of the sanctuary. Spend some time having the pastors and worship leaders mingle with the children. Divide the children into groups of no more than ten. Have youth and adults that the children love and trust head up these groups for an honest conversation time. Ask children to tell the leaders what components in the worship service help them worship God and what might be added. Assure the children that their names will not be called out when the list is shared in the large group. When the large group comes back together, have persons read the lists and compile one large list for the pastors and worship leaders. Ask the pastors and worship leaders to commit to gradually incorporating the ideas of the children in the worship service.

Here are some ideas that the children might suggest:

1. Children serve Communion occasionally. Training is required.
2. Sing a children's song or praise chorus once a month.
3. Start children's worship bags with children's bulletins.
4. Read the Scripture from a children's Bible once a month.
5. Have a puppet presentation in worship quarterly.
6. Let the children's choir sing regularly.
7. Begin a liturgical dance team.
8. Allow children to decorate the altar at least twice a year.
9. Hold a Children's Sabbath where children take all of the parts in the service.
10. Use prayers in the service occasionally that are written and read by children.
11. Preach a sermon occasionally that uses vocabulary and themes children understand.
12. Have children come forward near the baptismal font when a baby is baptized.
13. Offer a study for children on worship.
14. Let an older elementary child occasionally share a testimony of how God is working in his or her life.

Serve lunch. Choose a child to offer a thank-you prayer for the food.

After lunch, have children go into the sanctuary for a worship service designed just for them. End the worship time by having children bring in the communion cloth and communion elements. Select children to serve communion to their friends.

Before dismissing, have the pastors and worship leaders covenant with the children to work to make the children's ideas a reality in the congregation. Decide as a children's ministry team how you will communicate these ideas to the church leaders. Talk to your pastors about holding a teacher session for church members that will help them understand the role of children in worship and their part in helping children practice Passionate Worship.

A Child Practices Passionate Worship

Objective:

The children will:
- Learn about Matthew 21:12-16.
- Learn about children who praised Jesus with Passionate Worship.
- Learn about ways to praise Jesus today with their Passionate Worship.

Bible Story:

Matthew 21:12-16: Children praise Jesus in the Temple.

Bible Verse:

From the mouths of babies and infants you've arranged praise for yourself.
Matthew 21:16

Focus for the Teacher

The Gospel of Matthew relates the poignant story of children praising Jesus in the Temple, an example of children offering Passionate Worship (Matthew 21:12-16). Jesus enters Jerusalem on a donkey, turns over the tables in the Temple area, and heals the blind and lame. The chief priests and teachers of the law encounter some children in the Temple who are shouting their praises of "hosanna," and these religious leaders are angry. Prior to this story, we read the story of Jesus entering Jerusalem on a donkey and hear the same shouts of "hosanna." Surely the children present in the Temple were also present with their families on that day Jesus rode triumphantly into Jerusalem. They were scattered among the crowd that waved palm branches and heralded Jesus as their antici-

pated Deliverer from Roman oppression. Now we find these same children in the Temple area still praising and shouting, long after the cries of the adults have ceased.

Impacted by the Palm Sunday incident, the children continue their praise of Jesus, carrying their shouts of "hosanna" into the Temple, the sanctuary of worship for the Jewish people. Their Passionate Worship is evident in their shouting forth loud praises as their worship flows from out of the streets of Jerusalem into the Temple area.

When the Temple authorities seek to stifle the cries of the children, Jesus silences their protests by reminding the religious leaders of the words of the psalmist declaring that

God ordains praise from the lips of children and infants (Psalm 8:2). The word *ordained** gives special meaning to the praise of children and infants. God orders, authorizes, decrees, confirms, and honors the worship of children. Furthermore, Jesus implies that children not only have the right to worship, but they have the God-given capacity to worship even if they are only small children.

One wonders where the parents of these children are. Perhaps the parents understand that the children's lives will not be in jeopardy if they shout their praises in the Temple, whereas the parents' lives would be in grave danger. Temple soldiers guard diligently during the time of Passover to ensure no political uprisings occur. The parents could lift up their voices in the streets, but it would be unwise and unsafe to do so in the Temple. The waving of palm branches, a national symbol of independence for the Jewish people, signals to the Roman authorities that Jesus is very popular, so well liked that the people seem to believe he is their hope for deliverance. Their actions herald a warning to Rome that the crowds who follow Jesus need to be watched closely, as their hatred of Rome could lead to rebellion. In a sense, these children offer praise on behalf of all of the people who place their hopes in this man Jesus for their liberation from Rome! Children demonstrate Passionate Worship on behalf of all those who are unable to lift their voices in praise. Here we discover an amazing but often neglected story about the Passionate Worship of Jesus by children.

Jesus does not neglect the worship of the children, however. He is quick to point out to the religious leaders that the children obey Jewish Scripture when they offer their praises. The religious authorities cannot argue when Jesus confronts them with words from the psalmist that validate the actions of the children. When the chief priests and teachers of the law ask Jesus, "Do you hear what these children are saying?" what they imply is that the children are disrupting the important events of Temple life. These children whom the religious leaders view as unruly, Jesus views as worshiping children. The religious authorities hear only intrusive noise; Jesus hears joyful voices lifted in passionate praise.

Our congregations are filled with children who want to shout out their praises to Jesus but are often stopped by worship leaders and members who comprehend the intended worship of children as interruptions in worship. Children do not always worship in the way adults find acceptable. Children sometimes worship with loud singing, with bodies in motion, and with hands lifted in the air. Children worship by waving to friends for affirmation during children's sermons, by drawing a picture of the pastor during Communion, or by loudly whispering a question to parents during the pastor's sermon. Children participate in

If your congregation is a place filled with passionate worshipers, leaders will not try to stifle the voices of children like the religious leaders tried to do in the Temple.

*The New International Version of the Bible uses the word *ordained* whereas the CEB uses the word *arranged*.

Passionate Worship when they can touch the bread, hold the Bible, have the lines of the hymns traced for them by caring fingers, kneel at the altar, sing in the children's choir, light the altar candles, watch a video presentation, color a children's bulletin, or fold their hands in prayer. Children practice Passionate Worship best when they are allowed to use their senses in worship.

Just because children fail to worship in the same manner as adults or youth does not mean they are not passionate worshipers. Often rich, meaningful, Passionate Worship for children takes place when they leave the sanctuary and go to their own children's worship. Here the church gives them permission to worship in ways that children like to worship. In a worship time designed just for them, they sing joyful songs about God, Jesus, and the church; they make a craft that reinforces their lesson; they watch a puppet presentation based on a Bible story; they laugh at a silly game; and they dance to Christian music about God's love. Their senses come alive, they engage in worship, and God delights in their passionate praise. Yet the quality children's church experience does not substitute for or compensate for the failure of responsibility of church members to welcome children in the sanctuary and model for children Passionate Worship.

When children come into the sanctuary, the symbols of the church capture their attention and draw them into the holiness of the house of God. Here they view the cross and they are taught that Jesus loves the little children. Their eyes move to the altar, where a special book, a holy book, the Bible, rests. They are enthralled watching the acolytes light the altar candles. In some churches, the stories of the faith are etched into stained glass windows, pictures that reinforce the stories children learn in Sunday school. Children delight in colorful pastor's stoles, bright choir robes, needlepoint altar cushions, chrismon trees, and church-season-decorated altars. They savor the aroma of freshly baked Communion bread and cannot resist the temptation to dip their bread until their fingers touch the Communion juice. They stand, sit, sing, and pray not because these are merely the rote routines of worship, but because they are meaningful traditions in a place where children find great comfort, security, and love. Whether they realize it or not, God captures them with the gift of grace and provides them with the gift of a community of faith.

Here in this community of faith, these passionate child worshipers raise their voices like the child worshipers in the Jerusalem Temple raised their voices to praise Jesus. If your congregation is a place filled with passionate worshipers, leaders will not try to stifle the voices of children like the religious leaders tried to do in the Temple. Rather, imagine the jubilant voices of other worshipers in your congregation as they harmonize beautifully with the voices of children, as together all of God's children practice Passionate Worship that is both good and pleasing to God.

Passionate Worship

Welcome the Children to Passionate Worship

Welcome each child by name. As children arrive, give them a scarf to wave as they dance or move to praise songs appropriate for preschool children. Remind the children that they are praising God.

When children tire, have them sit down on a rug and sing some praise choruses. You may wish to invite your children's music director to come into the room and assist the children in singing.

Share the Bible Story (Matthew 21:12-16)

Invite a storyteller to come to your room to tell the Bible story, "Hear the Children Shout" (see page 44).

Reinforce the Story

Let the children pretend they are the children in the Temple praising Jesus. Teach them how to shout "hosanna" and practice this several times with the children.

Have a person dress in a biblical costume to represent Jesus. Instruct him to enter the classroom and greet the children. Have the children shout "hosanna" over and over again.

Have some persons dress in biblical costumes to represent the religious leaders. Direct them to enter the classroom and tell Jesus to stop the voices of the children. Have Jesus affirm the children and bless each child in the classroom.

Make a Communion Tablecloth

Have the children make a Communion cloth for the altar table in the sanctuary. Have a white piece of cloth that is hemmed and is the right size for your Communion table.

Prepare

Provide brightly colored scarfs, a CD of preschool praise music, and a CD player.

Prepare

Recruit someone to tell the story.

Photocopy the Bible story script on page 44.

Provide a Bible-times costume and a real or paper palm branch.

Prepare

Recruit an adult to portray Jesus and two or three adults to be Temple leaders.

Provide Bible-times costumes.

Purchase sponges in the shape of Christian symbols. If symbol sponges are not available, cut regular sponges into simple shapes such as a heart or cross.

Place folded paper towels in a shallow tray. Pour washable paint onto the paper towels to make a paint pad.

Instruct the children to wear smocks. Show the children how to dip their sponges in paint and stamp them on the cloth. Help the children wash their hands before removing their smocks.

Let the children present their Communion cloth to the pastor and remind him or her to use the cloth on the altar table for Communion Sunday and share with the congregation this gift from the preschool children.

Play Musical Instruments

Hand out musical instruments to each child. Play praise choruses or songs and let the children play their musical instruments. Encourage the children to sing along with songs that they know.

Passionate Worship During Snack Time

Hand out the snacks, but tell children to wait before eating their snack. Encourage each child to get down on bended knees and fold their hands in prayer. Say the prayer, "God is great, God is good, let us thank God for our food. Amen."

Practice Passionate Worship With a Parade

Let the preschoolers have a Passionate Worship parade. Make colorful streamers for each child. Tear crepe paper streamers into lengths of about eighteen inches. Twist one end of three or four of the streamers together and secure with tape. Lead the children as they march around the church shouting, "Hosanna!"

Closing Prayer

Jesus, we love you. Hosanna to Jesus. Amen.

Prepare

Provide a white cloth for the Communion table.

Provide paint smocks, washable paint, shallow trays, paper towels, sponges in the shape of Christian symbols, and hand-washing supplies.

Prepare

Provide musical instruments appropriate for preschoolers, a CD of preschool praise music, and a CD player.

Prepare

Provide simple snacks, juice, napkins, and cups. Be aware of any food allergies.

Prepare

Provide crepe paper streamers and tape.

Elementary

Passionate Worship

Welcome the Children to Passionate Worship

Welcome the children by name. As the children arrive direct their attention to a line you have attached from one chair to another. On this rope, clothespin copies of the church border (page 45).

As each child arrives, allow him or her to go to the rope and take one picture. Have him or her draw something that is in your church's sanctuary. It might be the altar, a candle, a symbol, or a stained-glass window.

Or have the children draw someone who leads in worship, such as a pastor, choir director, choir member, acolyte, or organist.

Clothespin the finished pictures back on the line.

Share the Bible Story (Matthew 21:12-16)

Recruit some of the youth in your church to come to your classroom and present the Bible story (see page 44) using puppets. If you do not have puppets available (Jesus, children, religious leaders) you can have the youth act this out as a skit.

Repeat the puppet presentation or skit, letting children in your classroom play the part of the children.

Teach the Children About Passionate Worship

Give the children the handout with the word *passionate* (see page 46). Have the children trace the word with crayons. Explain to the children that being passionate means you really love something, that something you do makes you very happy or fills you with great joy. Worship means to offer our praise to God.

Encourage the children to think of ways they worship God that make them feel happy, that give them great joy. Write each idea the children

Prepare

Photocopy the church border (page 45) for each child.

Attach a rope or string between two chairs like a clothesline.

Provide clothespins and crayons or markers.

Prepare

Photocopy "Hosanna, Hosanna" (page 44).

Recruit youth to present the script.

Provide puppets or simple Bible-times costumes.

Prepare

Photocopy the word Passionate *on page 46.*

Provide crayons, index cards, a marker, and clothespins.

Use the rope or string and church pictures displayed earlier.

share on a separate index card. Let the children clothespin the index cards to the line with their church pictures. Explain that their ideas of what makes them happy and joyful in worship equal Passionate Worship.

Practice Passionate Worship

Gather the children near the area where you have the line attached to the two chairs. Hand out the church pictures they made earlier.

Have each child hold up his or her picture to show to the other children. Encourage the child to tell about the picture. Discuss how each item pictured is used in worship or how each person pictured can help the children worship God. Then have the child hang the picture back on the rope.

Give each child a musical instrument. Point to a picture on your rope and say what this picture represents. Then have the children play their musical instruments and shout, "Hosanna!"

Read what the children have written on the index cards. Again, have the children play their musical instruments and shout, "Hosanna!" after you read each one.

Passionate Worship Charade Game

Let the children act out the role of worship leaders or ways they worship God in your worship service. Play worship charades by whispering in the ear of the child what they are to act out for the other children. The child who guesses correctly what the leader is acting out then becomes the leader.

Ideas for Worship Charade Game:
1. Reading the Bible
2. Singing
3. Praying
4. Pastor preaching sermon
5. Choir director as he or she directs the choir
6. Acolyte lighting the candles
7. Communion
8. Kneeling at the altar
9. Baptism of a baby
10. Playing of handbells

Serve Home-Baked Bread and Juice

As the children eat the home-baked bread, remind them of the bread they eat and the juice they drink together with their church friends when they come for Holy Communion. Remind the children that they remember Jesus during this special meal we call Communion or the Lord's Supper. Tell them that this can be a passionate time to worship God. Remember to say a thank-you prayer.

Passionate Worship Matching Cards Game

Divide the children into teams of two. Have each team place all the cards face-down. Let the children take turns selecting two cards. If the two cards match, the child can keep the cards. If they do not match, the child is to return the cards face-down. Play the game until all the cards have been matched.

Closing Prayer

Thank you, God, for our Bible story about the children who praised Jesus. Thank you that Jesus did not scold the children but knew that they were thanking God in ways that made them happy and filled them with joy. Help me to worship God in ways that make me happy and fill me with joy. In Jesus' name we pray. Amen.

Prepare

Provide juice, homemade bread, napkins, and cups.

Prepare

Photocopy and cut apart the matching cards on page 47. Two copies will make one set of cards. You will need one set for each pair of children. Shuffle each set.

Passionate Worship

Welcome the Children to Passionate Worship

Welcome the children by name. Have two or three listening centers around the room with a CD player and a CD of contemporary Christian music. Let the children choose a center and listen quietly to music.

Bible Study (Matthew 21:12-16)

Select a tween to read the Bible story. Divide the tweens into three groups. Select one tween in each group to be the recorder. Have the tweens use their Bibles and work together to answer the questions.

Group One: Jesus
1. How did Jesus react to the children shouting "Hosanna"?
2. What was Jesus doing in the Temple?
3. List ways that you worship God and Jesus that fill you with joy and make you want to shout "Hosanna."

Group Two: Religious Leaders
1. What was the reaction of the religious leaders to the children?
2. What else in our story made the religious leaders angry?
3. List honest reasons why some persons in your church may criticize children when they worship.

Group Three: Children
1. Write down some words that you think might describe the emotions of the children as they praised Jesus in the Temple.
2. Where do you think these children came from? Where were their parents?
3. Think of all the ways you see children in your own congregation praising God like the children in the Temple.

Come back together and share the tweens' reactions to the Bible story.

Prepare

Provide two or three CDs of contemporary Christian music and two or three CD players.

Prepare

Provide Bibles, paper, and pens or pencils.

Putting the Bible Story Into Action

Give each tween the symbols (page 47) and ask him or her to select one or two symbols that are meaningful in his or her faith journey.

Have each tween cut out those particular symbols and glue them on the shoe box. Have the tweens write down on index cards their suggestions on ways to improve the worship experience of children in the congregation. Explain to the tweens that their ideas should reflect ways for children to worship God with the same joy and enthusiasm as the children in the Temple. Place the index cards in the box and present it to your worship leaders.

Understanding Passionate Worship

Give each student a letter square to decorate with glitter. For example, one student will decorate the P, one the A, one the S, and so forth until all the letters in the word *passionate* are covered with glitter. If you have more than ten students, tweens can work in groups of two or more. After the letters are decorated, arrange them on a table to spell the word *passionate*. Once the glitter dries, hang the words on the wall.

Write on newsprint phrases that describe the word *passionate*. Some you might use are: "crazy about," "love with all of my heart," "excited about," "makes me joyful," "makes me very happy," and "yearn after."

Have the tweens cut out from magazine pictures things or events that they are passionate about. Glue them on a piece of posterboard to make a collage. Talk about some of the events or things in society that tweens are passionate about today.

Ask: "What are you passionate about here at church? What practices in our sanctuary draw you closer to God, excite you about your faith, and help you worship God?"

The Church Seasons and Passionate Worship

Each church season offers the opportunity for tweens to engage in Passionate Worship. Help the tweens explore Passionate Worship during the church seasons. Before class, gather items from your church or home to symbolize all the church seasons. Place these in a large container.

Prepare

Wrap a shoe box in wrapping paper. Wrap the lid separately.

Photocopy the symbols on page 47 for each tween.

Provide scissors, glue, index cards, and pens or pencils.

Prepare

Write the word passionate *in large bubble letters on posterboard. Cut out each letter in a square.*

Provide scissors, glitter, glue, tape, newsprint and markers, magazines, and posterboard.

Prepare

Provide items to represent each season (see list), and a large container.

Photocopy "Church Seasons" (page 48) for every five tweens.

Here are some ideas for items for your church season container:
- Advent: purple cloth, chrismons, Advent wreath, purple candles
- Christmas: white cloth, nativity scene
- Epiphany: green cloth, star, wise men, crown
- Lent: purple cloth, cross, crown of thorns, ashes, large nails, bread and cup (Jesus' Last Supper)
- Easter: white cloth, butterfly, silk lily, plastic egg, stuffed baby animals
- Pentecost: red cloth, plastic or wooden church, dove, red streamers
- Ordinary Time: green cloth, globe, clock, calendar

Divide the tweens into groups of five. Give each group the reproducible page on the church seasons (page 48). Assign each group a different season and have them read about that season in their group.

Let them take turns selecting items out of the container that fit their church season. Have a table or tables available for each group to set up their own church season display.

After the displays are complete, have each group tell the class about their display. Encourage the tweens to share ways they engage in Passionate Worship during each church season.

Plan a Passionate Worship Service

Let tweens plan their own Passionate Worship service. Have one tween write a call to worship. Ask several tweens to work together to write a creed, a statement telling what they believe about their faith. Allow the tweens to select their own music to play or sing and their own Scripture readings. Select a tween to say the prayer. Ask a few tweens to write about and be willing to talk about their faith for the sermon time. Practice the service. Set a date and invite your church worship leaders and their parents to come for a tween-led Passionate Worship experience.

Closing Prayer

Thank you for our Bible story about the children who praise you through Passionate Worship. Thank you, God, that you are always present with us when we worship you. We pray that we can honor you with Passionate Worship. We offer our prayer in the name of Jesus. Amen.

Prepare

Provide Bibles, hymnals, paper, and pens or pencils.

Families Can Teach Children Passionate Worship

Children mimic parents in the ways they worship. Children are keen observers and willing imitators of the ways others worship in their faith community, but they especially watch and observe family members. Families who engage in the practice of Passionate Worship teach children that the true worship of God fills the worshiper with great joy and sincere delight in God's presence. How do families demonstrate Passionate Worship to children? Children observe family members enjoying the experience of worship. Their faces contain happy expressions rather than looks of boredom. Families are faithful and diligent in worship attendance not just because this practice instills in their children a disciplined habit, but also because they love God's house, they love fellow worshipers, and they love to worship God. Children observe family members greeting other children and welcoming them to worship in the sanctuary. Rather than criticize the pastor or others, these family members extend appreciation to worship leaders in the presence of their children.

Family members who are passionate worshipers teach their children how to worship God beyond the bounds of the church building. These families engage in prayers at meal times, bedtime, and other times during the day. They lift up church members and friends who are ill or face difficulties in life. They offer heartfelt prayers and model the importance of a life of prayer. Families set aside time to make family devotionals a priority in the midst of busy schedules. Family conversations often turn to talks around God. Family activities point out God's creative hand in the world and God's wonderful and special plan for each child created in God's image.

Suggestions for Ways Families Can Practice Passionate Worship

1. Model for children regular attendance at worship.
2. Talk with children about worship. Talk with children about children's worship and children's sermon time. Ask them questions.
3. Help children learn how to worship. Line out the words of hymns for them so they can follow along as the congregation sings. Help children find the Scriptures in their children's Bibles when Scriptures are read in worship.
4. Allow children to greet other worshipers, sign attendance pads, and place their offerings in the offering plate.
5. Affirm children when they serve as worship leaders.
6. Do not criticize pastors and worship leaders in front of children.
7. Model prayer for children and allow them to say prayers in the family.
8. Set aside a devotional time.
9. Read Bible stories to children at bedtime and let children say a bedtime prayer.
10. When you take walks as a family or engage in outside activities, talk with children about God's beautiful world.

Stories of Children
Practicing Passionate Worship

Trenholm Road United Methodist in Columbia, South Carolina, offers children's church for the four- and five-year-old students. During the children's church period, for three weeks the children experience lessons that teach them the importance of Communion. They also learn how to take Communion. The fourth week, the children return to the service and the pastor invites them, as a class, to come forward and partake. This time represents a holy moment for the children and for the congregation. The children engage in Passionate Worship through the act of Holy Communion.

The pastor of Dumbarton United Methodist, Washington, D.C., preached a series of sermons on less-well-known women of the Bible. Her sermon on Lydia coincided with Communion Sunday. When the time arrived in the worship service for Communion, several children walked forward carrying a purple cloth. They carefully draped the cloth on the round Communion table in the center of the sanctuary. Two children processed in carrying the Communion elements, one the bread and one a chalice that contained the juice. They reverently placed the elements on the table. Then the worshipers gathered around the table to share together in remembering Christ's sacrifice. Both the children and the congregation engaged in Passionate Worship that morning.

The children's ministry team at Calvary United Methodist, Normal, Illinois, created the Family Prayer Room for children and their families. This is a place where children feel comfortable to share prayers either alone with God, with their families, or with a group of peers and leaders. Children remove their shoes as they enter this sacred space. There, children are captivated by the multi-sensory space, which includes unique scents, tastes of bread and fruit, clay to mold, and floor-to-ceiling canvas on which they write, draw, and color their prayers to our Lord. Children's leaders find the prayers of the children inspiring to read. Some children share painful words that bring tears to many eyes, while others rejoice over answered prayers. Children are able to connect with God in passionate prayer.

The children at Dumbarton United Methodist, Washington, D.C., usually leave the worship service for children's worship. When a liturgical dancer led in worship, the children were invited to remain in the sanctuary. The children were enthralled as they watched the dancer. Their faces lit up and they worshiped. They connected with God in a passionate way.

Children at Trenholm Road United Methodist, Columbia, South Carolina, do not just observe worship; instead, they are welcomed participants. Children are invited to serve as lay readers throughout the year, not just on Children's Sunday. Children take this responsibility seriously and are more involved in worship when they are given opportunities for service. Children are selected as worship helpers for special services such as Ash Wednesday.

Hear the Children Shout
by Daphna Flegal

(Enter waving palm branch and dancing around the room. Pretend to ignore the children, weaving in and out among them.)

Hosanna! Hosanna! Ho— Oh! Hello. I'm sorry, I didn't see you. I guess I wasn't watching where I was going. I'm just so excited. I just saw Jesus! He came into town riding on a donkey. Did you see him? Well, I sure did. I stood on the side of the road waving my palm branch and shouting, "Hosanna!"

Then I followed Jesus into the city. He went to the Temple. So many people came to the Temple to see him. Some of the people who came could not see—and guess what? He touched them and made them see! Some of the people who came could not walk. But Jesus healed them and they started leaping and dancing around. *(Dance around.)*

And then the children came into the Temple. The children were so much fun to watch. They waved their palm branches and shouted, "Hosanna! Hosanna!" *(Wave the palm branch.)*

But the Temple leaders did not like what the children were doing. "Do you hear what these children are saying?" they asked Jesus angrily.

Jesus nodded his head. "Yes, I hear them," he said. "Remember, God wants even babies and infants to show praise."

Then Jesus left the Temple, but I can still hear the children shouting, "Hosanna! Hosanna!" Let's shout like the children in the Temple. Let's all shout, "Hosanna!" together. Hosanna! Hosanna! *(Encourage the children to shout with you.)*

Hosanna, Hosanna, Praise Jesus!
by Rita Hays

Children: Hosanna, hosanna, praise Jesus!

Religious Leader 1: Do you hear what those children are shouting?

Religious Leader 2: Yes, I do. They are praising Jesus and they are making too much noise. This is the Temple. These children need to be quiet.

Children: Hosanna, hosanna, praise Jesus!

Religious Leader 3 *(addressing Jesus)*: Jesus, do you hear what these children are shouting?

Jesus: Yes, I do.

Religious Leaders: Quiet them!

Jesus: In our Scriptures it is written that God approves of the worship of children. Psalm 8:2 says, "Out of the mouth of children, God commands praise." Why should I stop the children from worshiping God when God approves of their praise?

Children: Hosanna, hosanna, praise Jesus!

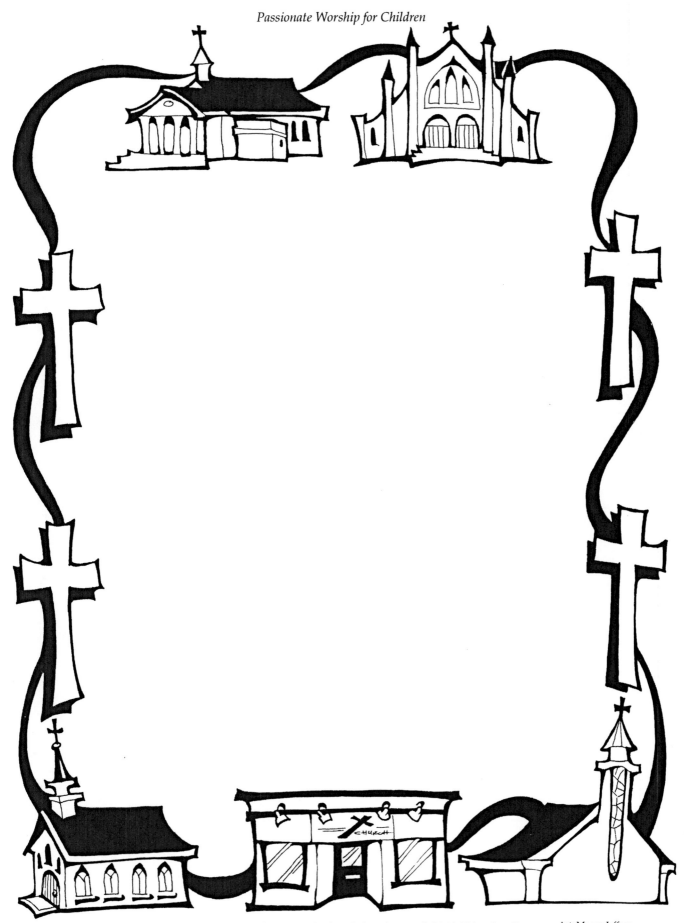

Art: Megan Jeffery
© 2005 Abingdon Press

Art: Susan Harrison
© 2005 Abingdon Press

Church Seasons

Advent

Four Sundays leading up to Christmas day.

We prepare for the birth of Christ. Purple is the color of royalty, so we use it during Advent to remind us that Jesus is our King. This is why an Advent wreath has four purple candles, although some churches use one pink candle, the joy candle. Some of the symbols for Advent are chrismons (symbols that teach us about Jesus) and the Advent wreath.

Christmas

Twelve days beginning with Christmas day.

We celebrate the birth of Christ. White is the bright color of this season as it reminds us that Jesus is the light of the world. One of the most important symbols of Christmas is the nativity scene showing Mary, Joseph, baby Jesus, the shepherds, and the animals.

Epiphany

Epiphany begins on January 6 and goes until Lent.

We remember the wise men and their gifts of gold, frankincense, and myrrh. Green is the color because it reminds us of growth. Because the wise men were not Jewish, we remember that God's love is for all people. Symbols of Epiphany include: crown, star, and wise men.

Lent

Six Sundays before Easter Day.

We recall the stories in the Bible of Jesus riding into Jerusalem on a donkey as persons waved palm branches (Palm Sunday), Jesus sharing the Last Supper with his disciples, and Jesus dying on the cross. We use the color purple during Lent as it represents our attempts to grow in our faith and think seriously about our faith. Lent begins with Ash Wednesday. An Ash Wednesday service, where ashes are placed on the forehead of each person, reminds us we need to tell God we are sorry for our sins. Some of the symbols of Lent are: ashes, crown of thorns, donkey, palm branch, nails, cross, bread and cup.

Easter

Easter Sunday and the six following Sundays.

Jesus is risen! The color for Easter is white to celebrate the Resurrection. The symbols remind us of new life and include: butterflies, lilies, eggs, and baby animals.

Pentecost

Fifty days after Easter.

We celebrate the birthday of the Church. Pentecost recalls the story in Acts where the Holy Spirit came "as flames of fire." We use a red cloth to represent the flames of fire. Some of the symbols are: church, dove (represents the Holy Spirit). Streamers remind us that this is a happy, joyful season.

Ordinary Time

The time between Pentecost and Advent.

We remember that God is with us not only during the holy, special times of the church year, but in the ordinary days as well. Some of the symbols are: globe (God is at work in the world), calendar, and clock (God is in charge of our time).

3.

Intentional Faith Development for Children

Introduction

Third-grader Carlos Sanchez proudly receives his third-grade Bible during the worship service at his church. Carlos understands the importance of daily Bible readings and rigorous lifetime dedication to the study of God's Word. When the pastor asks the congregation to turn in their Bibles to the sermon text for the message, Carlos easily finds the Scripture passage and happily follows along as the pastor reads. Carlos's church takes time to equip their third-graders so they are prepared to use their Bibles adequately when they receive them as a gift from the church.

Carlos's church invites and encourages all third-graders to attend a "Get to Know Your Bible" day at the church. Through fun games, Bible-related crafts, and enjoyable Scripture activities, the third-graders learn about the Bible and how to use it. When the pastor presents the Bible to third-graders, those children who attended the "Get to Know Your Bible" day already know the sections of their Bible and how to look up Scripture passages. Their new Bible holds greater value and deeper meaning for Carlos and his friends because his church engages the third-graders

in a well-planned, high-quality Intentional Faith Development event that targets the developmental level of third-graders.

Sixth-grader Sally Sparks cherishes the time spent in her confirmation class. She eagerly looks forward to each session. Pastors and mentors sincerely care about the faith development of their sixth-graders and start meeting and planning weeks before the confirmation class gathers. As a leadership team, they engage in detailed planning that ensures that confirmation remains a high-quality yet enjoyable experience year after year. Sally notices that her pastors find creative and unique ways to share the confirmation materials with the class. She appreciates the field trips the class embarks upon as they travel to churches of religious backgrounds different from her own United Methodist heritage. When they attend worship at locations other than their own church, Sally notes that she and her friends gain a greater respect and fuller appreciation for differing faith traditions. Their mission project to serve a meal at the local homeless shelter excites Sally and expands her perspective on homelessness. Sally thanks God for her loving, affirming mentor, who engages her in lively discussions and honestly talks with her as she struggles with faith issues.

Sally belongs to a church that insists parents and students make confirmation a priority in their busy schedules. Sally worships in a congregation where leaders lift up the confirmation class daily in their prayers. Sally attends a church where pastors and mentors prepare diligently for the confirmation classes. Sally values her confirmation experience because her congregation values her faith journey and takes painstaking efforts to plan and produce a high-quality, well-planned, Intentional Faith Development experience that targets the developmental needs of sixth-graders.

Churches that take seriously the Wesleyan concept of grace understand, accept, and appreciate their role as intentional faith developers for children. Wesleyan theology teaches about a God who reaches out to, extends love to, and claims each of us as God's own precious, beloved child (prevenient grace). However, in order for children to come to the pivotal point in their faith journey where they can say a resounding "yes" to God's gracious gift of salvation and claim for themselves the traditions and teachings of the faith (justifying grace), they must be taught and nurtured through various experiences of Intentional Faith Development. Then, equipped with the tools of the faith, these lifetime learners continue to grow and develop in their faith (sanctification) in large part because of congregations that covenant to mold, shape, strengthen, and nurture them. Their educating faith communities believe in and practice Intentional Faith Development that spans from birth to death.

What is Intentional Faith Development?
What does it have to do with children?

A church's concept of its role in Intentional Faith Development begins with members' efforts to model themselves after the Master Teacher. In Scripture, those who encounter Jesus do not address him by the title of "preacher"; they refer to him as rabbi or teacher. Jesus appears in the biblical text as a persuasive teacher who captures his audience with stories about the kingdom of God. Jesus understands his audience and uses excellent teaching methods. He selects illustrations his listeners relate to: lost coins, found sheep, and shrewd landowners. Jesus chooses subjects familiar to his students: sheep on a hillside, grapevines, farmers, seed, and soil. Jesus intrigues his hearers by inviting them to "sell all they have and give to the poor" or "take up your cross and follow me." Jesus teaches and models Intentional Faith Development.

Intentional Faith Development takes time and dedication on the part of church leaders. There is no room for hectic last-minute planning, haphazard schedules, and frantic, harried leaders. Priority must be given to meeting age-level needs. Leaders work for quality results. Honest follow-up evaluations provide necessary feedback for future endeavors.

Excellent Intentional Faith Development produces fruitful results. First, it leads persons to faith in Jesus Christ and helps individuals mature in their faith. Second, it offers persons the opportunity to grow in community and fellowship with other Christians who nurture and affirm one another. Intentional Faith Development works best in community with other Christian believers. Third, Intentional Faith Development forms disciples for Jesus Christ. Congregations send these trained disciples forth from their churches into the world.

Intentional Faith Development offers boundless opportunities for persons to expand their faith experiences. Never limited to church spaces, Intentional Faith Development can take place both inside and outside the walls of the church. It can be as traditional as Sunday school classes, choirs, Disciple classes, parenting and marriage classes, and church retreats, or as non-traditional as prayer groups on the web, mid-week lunch support groups, Facebook faith discussions, and off-site Bible studies. Good leaders always keep in mind the main goals. The purpose of Intentional Faith Development remains the same as the mission of the church: to reach persons for Christ, make disciples, and send equipped persons out into the world.

Children's lives change and they mature spiritually when the church invests in Intentional Faith Development that targets their developmental needs at each stage of physical, spiritual, and emotional growth. Each age deserves Intentional Faith Development. Without it their growth in faith will remain shallow, undernourished, and misguided. What an awesome responsibility to impact our children with good, solid Intentional Faith Development!

Picture what Intentional Faith Development looks like in a congregation that takes seriously its task to nurture children. Children arrive at Sunday school classes in which trained teachers greet them by name, use quality curriculum in their classes, and motivate students to learn. Vacation Bible school becomes a community outreach endeavor and children are eager to return year after year. Confirmation classes invigorate the students and challenge them to continue their faith journey. Church camp, children's choirs, children's handbell choirs, children's Christmas drama, mission projects, retreats, and special studies are all excellent and vital ways to deepen the faith of children when they are planned and carried out intentionally. Friendships form as together children learn, children change, children grow, and children share. Enthusiastic children proudly want to invite other children to join them.

Intentional Faith Development impacts children with lasting results.

When we produce Intentional Faith Development programs, studies, and events in our congregations, they become healthier places for children to worship, to learn, and to serve. Children yearn to join in community and fellowship with other believers. They want to study God's Word and apply it to their lives. They like to be asked to share in mission projects that help those in need. They desire to use their gifts in the body of Christ. Intentional Faith Development opportunities open the door for them to do all of these things and more.

We do well to remember that we serve a Master Teacher who models for us Intentional Faith Development and guides us at all times, in all circumstances, and in all places. The Master Teacher asks us to be faithful and calls us to the highest standards of excellence. Our children deserve our best efforts. Our only reward comes when we hear the Master Teacher proclaim, "Well done, good and faithful servant."

Workshop for Lesson Three

Encourage the members of your children's ministry team, your Sunday school teachers, and other volunteers in your children's ministry area to gather for a time of teaching and reflection on the ways children in your church may be involved in practices of Intentional Faith Development.

Prayer and Welcome

Reflections on Luke 2:41-51

Since this Scripture presents the story of the time in which Jesus becomes separated from his parents, participants need time to discuss that aspect of the story before moving to the incident of Jesus in the Temple with the teachers. Look ahead in the next section of your curriculum and read the author's discussion under "A Child Practices Intentional Faith Development" (Focus for the Teacher).

Divide the group into two teams. After discussion, each team should choose one person to portray Mary and one to portray Jesus and write a dialogue that the persons portraying Mary and Jesus will share with the group.

Team One: Take the viewpoint of Mary.

1. Describe how you think Mary feels when she realizes her son is missing.
2. Describe how you think Mary feels when she finds Jesus.
3. Describe how you think Mary feels when Jesus gives his reasons for wanting to be in the Temple.
4. Describe how you think Mary feels when she returns home, observes Jesus' obedience, and watches his growth.

Team Two: Take the viewpoint of Jesus.

1. Describe how you think Jesus feels in the Temple among the teachers.
2. Describe how you think Jesus feels as a twelve-year-old boy when his mother arrives to take him home.
3. Describe how you think Jesus feels when he returns home.

Bring the teams back together as a group and have the persons portraying Mary and Jesus present their dialogues.

Divide again into two teams. Give each team a piece of paper, a flip chart, and a marker. One team is to write down questions they think Jesus might have asked the teachers in the Temple. The other team is to write down questions children might ask their teachers and church leaders in your church. Come back together and share your questions. If time permits, take time to share ways you might answer the questions of the children in your church.

Affirm the Ways Your Children Now Engage in Intentional Faith Development

Take some time to share with the participants the difference between generic faith development and Intentional (well-planned and well-executed) Faith Development. Ask them to brainstorm about all the ways your children engage in Intentional Faith Development in your church. Write these down on a flip chart as persons call them out.

Give each person a cut-out pattern of a church. Read out one at a time the ways your children engage in Intentional Faith Development and point to someone whom you assign to write down that particular program/event on her or his church cut-out.

After participants list ways of Intentional Faith Development on their cut-out churches, glue the cut-outs on circular wreaths. After the wreaths are complete, pass them out among the participants. Let individuals lay hands on the wreaths and thank God for the ways of Intentional Faith Development in your church. Decorate each wreath with a bow and hang them in the children's area.

Where to Go From Here?

Share the teaching materials in this chapter that are designed for a Sunday school lesson, children's worship lesson, or special teaching session. There are teaching materials for separate use with preschool, elementary, and older elementary (tween) children. Decide as a group how and when you will teach this material to the children. Set a date for the teaching of these lessons. After the lessons are taught, determine how you might initiate at least one new Intentional Faith Development program or event for the children at your church.

Ask teachers to take time in elementary and older elementary Sunday school classes to ask the children to think of new ideas for Intentional Faith Development, or you may do this as you are teaching these lessons.

After the lessons are taught and/or children share their creative ideas for new programs/events, determine how you will select which ideas to put into practice in your congregation. Talk with your pastor(s) and include other church leaders in your discussions. Invite representative elementary and older children to share the ideas of their age groups. Decide as a group what new Intentional Faith Development idea you will begin in your church.

Some Ideas for Intentional Faith Development

1. Kid's Club (activities for older elementary children)
2. Weekly Bible study for older elementary boys/girls
3. New children's worship format
4. Mission project for children
5. Vacation Bible school for an inner-city church
6. Pre-school activities
7. Introduction of curriculum in the nursery area
8. Mission study for children
9. Discipleship training class for children
10. Children's choir or children's handbell choir
11. Acolyte training program with consecration of acolytes in worship
12. Course for children on worship
13. Training program for children to serve in worship as greeters, ushers, and Scripture readers
14. Children's Sabbath (Sunday when children offer leadership roles in worship)
15. Stewardship training for children
16. Mid-week program for children

Celebrate and Affirm the Ideas of Children

Host a picnic for your pastors and church leaders. Select a park or your own picnic shelter. If the weather is bad, hold the picnic at the church. Invite children and their families to attend and bring a picnic lunch. Your committee will want to fix a picnic lunch for the pastors and church leaders. Place their lunches in attractive picnic baskets and enclose in each picnic basket the new Intentional Faith Development project that you are starting for the children. Use the picnic time to discuss how to advertise and implement the new program/event. Celebrate and affirm all of the creative ideas of children and ask blessings upon the new Intentional Faith Development program/event.

A Child Practices Intentional Faith Development

Objective:

The children will:
- Hear Luke 2:41-51.
- Learn ways Jesus practiced Intentional Faith Development at the age of 12 years.
- Learn ways to practice Intentional Faith Development today.

Bible Story:

Luke 2:41-51: Jesus' parents hunt for Jesus when he becomes separated from his family on a return trip home from Jerusalem. His parents find Jesus in the Temple talking about faith matters with the religious teachers.

Bible Verse:

Everyone who heard him was amazed by his understanding and his answers.
Luke 2:47

Focus for the Teacher

Luke is the only Gospel writer who records this incident of Jesus getting lost and being found in the Temple. Without this story, we would lack an interesting insight into the desire of Jesus to engage in Intentional Faith Development at the age of twelve. We often fix our attention on the details of Jesus getting lost from his parents, so we fail to recognize the importance of Jesus' question-and-answer time with the religious teachers. In Jewish tradition, Jesus falls agewise on the brink of manhood. Perhaps Jesus desires to learn all he can from the religious teachers and realizes that this is a golden opportunity for him to dialogue with them. This story gives us a glimpse into the emerging growth of Jesus and highlights his humanity.

Yet, before we get to the Intentional Faith Development angle in our story, we must get past Jesus being lost. On the surface, it appears to us that Jesus disobeys his parents, upsets them, makes an excuse for his actions, and embarrasses his mother. Honestly, most parents relate to this story because it sounds to them like a typical twelve-year-old! In reading the story, we keep before us a picture of both the humanity of Jesus and the divinity of Christ. We struggle at times in Scripture to know when one emerges and the other comes into play. We cannot solve this tension in our Gospel, and Luke does not intend for us to. Luke wants us to sense that the boy Jesus struggles with his own destiny and call as he grows from child to man.

It helps to examine the travel patterns of Jewish families in the time of Jesus. For safety, persons travel in caravans. Some men always go first, ahead of the other travelers, to provide protection. In the middle of the crowd are the women and children. Other men position themselves at the back of the pack. Jesus' attention remains so focused on his dialogue with the teachers that he apparently does not even think about his return family trip. Perhaps he reasons that his parents will find him when it is time to depart. In all honesty, Jesus wishes to stay in Jerusalem.

The return trip begins. His parents assume Jesus travels somewhere in the crowd of friends and relatives. Mary, traveling with the women and children, thinks Jesus is with the men; this is where he now belongs. Mary knows that soon her son will become an adult and likes to be treated as such. Joseph, who travels with the men, thinks Jesus is with the women, for surely his mother wants to hang on to his childhood for just a little longer. Parents today fail to perceive this kind of childcare arrangement, but in Jesus' time relatives and friends watched over children, relieving parents of some of the anxiety.

Readers of Luke's Gospel are quick to reprimand Mary and Joseph for waiting three days before they return to Jerusalem. Given the above scenario, they travel one day before they make camp and realize Jesus is missing. It takes them another day to travel back to Jerusalem, and on the third day they search for Jesus and finally find Jesus in the Temple. Upon finding Jesus, we often critically read into the text rudeness on Jesus'

part as he says to his mother, "Why were you searching for me?" Yet Jesus states the obvious. His parents do not need to search for him in the homes of relatives and friends in Jerusalem when it is obvious where he can be found. He reminds his mother of his true destiny and his need to be in the place where that destiny is shaped and nurtured.

Jesus struggles as a boy between conflicting loyalties and decides God comes first. No doubt Jesus' blunt honesty hurts Mary, just as the blunt honesty of our own children hurts us from time to time, but she recalls that she birthed no ordinary son. Luke softens the storyline when Jesus returns home, obeys his parents, and grows in wisdom and strength.

The boy Jesus practices Intentional Faith Development when he listens and asks questions.

Luke urges us to move ahead to the essential part of the story. The teachers help Jesus in his own Intentional Faith Development. Jesus seeks out those who can best nurture his faith and answer his questions. Teachers in the Temple sit in a circle with their students, where they engage them in conversations about religious matters. There remains a give-and-take in the dialogue, but apparently Jesus amazes the teachers with his knowledge of the Torah as he discusses with them. The boy Jesus practices Intentional Faith Development when he listens and asks questions.

These same methods apply today as we engage children in quality learning and Intentional Faith Development that excites them just as it inspired and delighted the young Jesus.

Preschool

Intentional Faith Development

Welcome the Children to Intentional Faith Development

Welcome each child by name. Give the children a Bible sticker to put on their clothes.

Enlist the help of a good reader. Have that person sit in a designated area in your classroom, and as the children arrive, have them join that person as he or she reads some children's Bible stories.

Share the Bible Story (Luke 2:41-51)

Gather the children and have them sit on a rug. Have the children imitate your motions to the Bible story. Repeat the story several times.

One day Jesus and his family were visiting friends in a large city. *(Shake hands with another child.)* Soon it was time for Jesus and his family to travel back to their home. *(Wave goodbye.)* Jesus got lost! *(Look down sadly.)* His mother found him in the Temple. *(Wave hands happily in the air.)* He was talking to the teachers and asking them some questions about God. *(Raise hands up above head.)*

Reinforce the Story

Invite the pastor to come to your classroom. Explain to the children that just like Jesus asked questions, you and the class are going to ask the pastor some questions. Talk with the children about some of the questions they might ask the pastor. These do not necessarily have to be questions of faith. They can be such questions as "Do you have a dog?" or "What is your favorite color?" Preschool children need to be comfortable talking with their pastor as a friend just as Jesus was comfortable talking with the teachers in the Temple.

Prepare

Provide Bible stickers and Bible storybooks.

Recruit a person to read Bible storybooks to the children.

Prepare

Arrange for a pastor to visit with the children.

The Bible Is a Special Book

Help the children to understand that the Bible is a special book that helps them learn about God and Jesus. Have the children sit in a circle. Give each child a small Bible to hold. Do the following actions with the children, and when you say a phrase, have the children repeat the phrase as a class.

1. Hold the Bible close to your heart—"I love the Bible."
2. Hold the Bible in the air—"I learn from the Bible."
3. Hold the Bible toward the teachers—"My teacher helps me learn."
4. Hold the Bible in your lap—"I love Bible stories."

Make Bibles Out of Play Dough

Let the children make Bibles out of play dough. Show the children how to flatten a piece of play dough and then fold it in half. Remind them that our Bible is a special book. We use our Bibles to learn about God and Jesus.

Snack Time

As the children eat their snack, play music that centers on Bible stories. Talk about the stories with the children.

Create a Special Bible Center

Remind the children that the Bible is a very special book. We need to take good care of our Bibles. Tell the children that they are going to help create a special place in your room for the Bible.

Set up a small round table to house your Bible. Let children decorate a cloth to fit on the table. The children may decorate the cloth with crayons or markers or by adding religious stickers. If you have religious stamps available, show the children how to press the stamps onto a nonpermanent stamp pad and then onto the tablecloth.

Allow the children to help you set up the Bible center. Place the cloth on the table. Bring the Bible to the center of the table and set it on a stand. Let the children take turns standing by the table and holding the Bible as you repeat today's Bible verse with each child.

Prepare

Provide a small Bible for each child.

Prepare

Provide play dough.

Prepare

Provide a simple snack, juice, napkins, and cups.

Provide a CD of preschool Bible story songs and a CD player.

Prepare

Provide a classroom Bible, book stand, small table, and paper tablecloth to fit the table, along with crayons, markers, religious stickers, or religious stamps and nonpermanent stamp pads.

Say a prayer thanking God for the Bible and the stories of the Bible.

Prayer: Dear God, thank you for our Bible and our Bible center in our
class. Thank you for Bible stories that teach us about God and
Jesus. Amen.

Sing About the Bible

Have the children sit in your Bible center. Sing the songs printed
below. Each song is sung to a familiar tune.

The Bible Is a Special Book
(Tune: Mary Had a Little Lamb)

The Bible is a special book,
special book, special book.
The Bible is a special book.
It says that God loves me.

Words: Elizabeth Crocker
© 1995 Cokesbury

Turn the Pages
(Tune: Twinkle, Twinkle, Little Star)

The Bible is a special book
Turn the pages, take a look.
Hear the stories that are there.
Learn about God's love and care.
The Bible is a special book
Turn the pages, take a look.

Words: Daphna Flegal
© 1997 Abingdon Press

A Special Book
(Tune: This Old Man)

Special book, special book,
the Bible is a special book.
With songs and poems and
            stories that are true,
the Bible says that God loves you.

Words: Daphna Flegal
© 1997 Abingdon Press

Look in the Bible
(Tune: Are You Sleeping?)

Look in the Bible, look in the Bible.
What do you see? What do you see?
Stories of God's love. Stories of
            God's love.
God loves me. God loves me.

Words: Daphna Flegal
© 1997 Abingdon Press

Closing Prayer

Thank you, God, for our story of Jesus. Jesus loved to learn about God.
Help us love to learn Bible stories about God just like Jesus. Amen.

Elementary

Intentional Faith Development

Welcome the Children to Intentional Faith Development

Greet each child by name. As children arrive, give them the Books of the Bible page (page 70). Have them glue the page onto construction paper and decorate the border.

Share the Bible Story (Luke 2:41-51)

Set up your room like a Temple area. Provide cushions for the children to sit on. Display some scrolls (paper attached to dowel rods, rolled up, and tied with a ribbon or string). Let the children dress in Bible costumes.

Gather the children and have them sit in the Temple area. Ask them to listen carefully to the story. Explain to them that they will play a game that asks questions about the story. Read it to them from a children's storybook or a children's Bible. Be sure to cover the facts needed to answer the game questions below. Take time to garner the reaction of the children to the story.

Reinforce the Story With a Game

Divide the children into two teams. Each team takes a turn pulling something out of the bag. If the child pulls out a fish, he or she may answer the question. If a child pulls out a shark, his or her team loses this turn and the other team gets the opportunity to draw from the bag. A child may answer a question only if he or she draws a fish. Each child should have a chance to draw from the bag. The winning team is the one that collects the most fish by the end of the game.

1. What city did Jesus and his family travel to? *(Jerusalem)*
2. How often did Jesus' family travel to Jerusalem? *(once a year)*

Prepare

Photocopy the Books of the Bible sheet (page 70) for each child.

Provide construction paper, glue, and colored pencils.

Prepare

Provide cushions, paper scrolls, biblical costumes, and a children's Bible or Bible storybook.

Prepare

Photocopy and cut out the fish and shark pictures on page 71. You will need 15 fish and at least 5 sharks.

Optional: laminate the fish and shark cut-outs.

Place the fish and shark cut-outs in a bag.

3. How old was Jesus in our Bible story for today? *(twelve years old)*
4. What happened to Jesus when his family left on their journey back to their home? *(He wasn't with them.)*
5. What are the names of Jesus' parents? *(Mary and Joseph)*
6. How many days did it take before Jesus was found? *(three)*
7. Where did his parents find Jesus? *(in the Temple)*
8. Who was Jesus with? *(the teachers)*
9. What was Jesus doing? *(listening and asking questions)*
10. How did the teachers respond to Jesus? *(They were amazed.)*
11. What did Mary ask Jesus? *(Why have you treated us like this? Didn't you know we would be worried?)*
12. How did Jesus reply? *(Did you not know that I would be in my Father's house?)*
13. What happened to Jesus after this? *(He returned home and was obedient to his parents.)*
14. What did Mary do? *(She treasured all of these things in her heart.)*
15. What book of the Bible tells our story for today? *(Luke)*

Teach the Children About Intentional Faith Development

Give the children the treasure boxes. Let the children decorate their boxes with stickers or felt decorations.

On a small piece of paper, have them write the words to Psalm 119:105 (NRSV): "Your word is a lamp to my feet and a light to my path."

Talk with the children about times when they walk in darkness and need a flashlight to help them see. Explain that in Bible times people used lamps to help them find their way in the darkness.

Tell the children that the Bible helps them, teaches them, and guides them. Encourage the children to use their Bibles to learn about God and Jesus. Remind them that the Bible helps them grow in their faith.

Have the children put the Scripture verses in their treasure boxes.

Learn the song "Thy Word Is a Lamp" (*The United Methodist Hymnal*, No. 601).

Prepare

Purchase a small treasure box for each child. They are available from www.oriental-trading.com.

Provide stickers or felt decorations and glue, paper, and pencils or pens.

Decorate Bible Covers

Give each child a Bible cover. Let the children use markers to decorate their Bible covers. Talk with the children about the care of their Bibles. Tell the children that the Bible is a very special book. Explain to the children why we call the Bible a holy book.

Learning to Use My Bible

Hand out Bibles to each child. Show the children how to find chapters and verses in the Bible. Teach them about the sections of the Bible using the page they decorated when they arrived for class. Let the children find some books in their Bible.

An excellent resource is *Learning to Use My Bible* by Joyce Brown (Abingdon Press, ISBN-13: 9780687645671).

Bible Snack Time

Serve snacks that Bible people ate, such as grapes, raisins, and bread. Talk about the kinds of foods that are mentioned in the Bible. Ask the children what kinds of food they think Jesus liked when he was a boy.

Pockets Magazine

Obtain a copy of *Pockets* magazine (Upper Room) for each child. If you do not subscribe to this magazine in your church, ask a church in your community to give you some of their extra copies. Let the children browse through the devotional magazine, read some of the articles, and work some of the activity pages. Let the children take the magazine home and encourage them to show it to their parents. Inform parents about the magazine when they arrive to pick up their children.

Closing Prayer

Thank you, God, for our lesson today about Jesus as a young boy. Thank you that Jesus wanted to be in the Temple to learn about God. Help us to always want to learn about God and Jesus. Thank you for our church. We are glad that we can come to our church and learn Bible stories. In Jesus' name. Amen.

Prepare

Purchase a Bible cover for each child. They are available from www.oriental-trading.com.

Provide markers.

Prepare

Provide Bibles for each child and the Books of the Bible pages used earlier.

Prepare

Provide raisins, grapes, bread, juice, napkins, and cups.

Prepare

Provide samples of Pockets. *Go to pockets.upper room.org for more information.*

Note: This is an excellent resource for children's Intentional Faith Development and parents may wish to purchase one for the child for his or her birthday or other special occasions.

Tween
(Older Elementary)

Intentional Faith Development

Welcome the Children to Intentional Faith Development

Welcome the children by name and direct them to a table for a Bible activity. On the table where the activity will take place, lay out the pieces of construction paper with "Old Testament" and "New Testament" written on them. Give the children the index cards labeled with the books of the Bible. Encourage the children to work together to put each book in the correct part of the Bible and then arrange the books in the proper order.

Bible Study (Luke 2:41-51)

Ask tweens to read the Bible story (Luke 2:41-51) with a partner. Provide various translations. Talk about the story and compare words in the various translations.

Divide the tweens into three groups.

- **Group One:** Write a rap to the Bible story.
- **Group Two:** Act the story out through mime.
- **Group Three:** Act the story out as a modern-day skit.

Bring the groups back together and have each of them share.

Reinforce the Bible Story

Encourage the tweens to write down some questions about their faith to ask their pastor. Give the questions to him or her and invite the pastor to attend a later class session to answer the questions and dialogue with the tweens.

Prepare

Write the name of each book of the Bible on a separate index card.

Write "New Testament" on one piece of construction paper and "Old Testament" on a second piece.

Prepare

Provide Bibles in different translations, paper, and pens or pencils.

Prepare

Provide paper and pens or pencils.

Understanding Intentional Faith Development

Prepare

Provide computers or dictionaries.

Provide newsprint, markers, pencils, construction paper, scissors, and tape.

If the tweens have access to computers, have them look up definitions using an online dictionary. If not, use a printed dictionary. Divide the tweens into three groups.
- **Group One:** Look up the meaning of *intentional*.
- **Group Two:** Look up the meaning of *faith*.
- **Group Three:** Look up the meaning of *development*.

Develop a class sentence that gives the meaning of Intentional Faith Development. An example might be: "Planned, purposeful study (intentional) to help shape a person's beliefs about God and Jesus (faith) and help him or her grow in faith (development)." Write this sentence on newsprint.

Give the tweens construction paper. Have the tweens cut large leaves out of the paper. Encourage the tweens to list all of the many ways they see Intentional Faith Development taking place for children and write these on the leaves.

Let the tweens help you make a tree without leaves using construction paper. Mount this tree on the wall. Have tweens tape their leaves to the tree.

Practice Intentional Faith Development

Prepare

Provide newsprint and markers.

Encourage the tweens to brainstorm about new ideas for Intentional Faith Development. Tell them these ideas will be shared at a picnic with church leaders.

Intentional Faith Development and the Bible

Prepare

Provide the Books of the Bible cards made earlier.

Have the tweens return to the tables where they started during the welcome time. Look at all of the books in the Bible. Have the tweens count to discover how many books are in the Old Testament and how many are in the New Testament. Briefly explain each section of the Bible, and as you share the name of that section, have one tween read the names of the books found in that section.

Intentional Faith Development and the Ten Commandments

Read the Ten Commandments listed in Exodus 20:2-17 and in Deuteronomy 5:6-21. Remind the tweens that the Ten Commandments provide an excellent guide to help them in their efforts at Intentional Faith Development.

Give each tween a copy of the stone tablet page (page 72). Have the tweens write the Ten Commandments on their tablets and then glue the Ten Commandments on wood or cardboard to make plaques. Let the tweens paint over the paper with the glue mixture. The tweens may take the plaques home after they are dry.

Intentional Faith Development Calendar

Give each tween a calendar page and one page of each kind of sticker. Encourage the tweens to practice habits of Intentional Faith Development outside of church time. Every time during the month they engage in one of the faith practices, they should put a sticker on their calendar for that day.
   • Time spent in prayer: praying hands sticker
   • Time spent reading the Bible: Bible sticker
   • Time spent _____ (*let each tween decide her or his own faith practice*): cross sticker

If you cannot find religious stickers, use other stickers, such as different-colored stars.

Intentional Faith Development in Other Traditions

Take the tweens to a worship service in a Jewish synagogue. Since the services are held on Friday evening, tweens will not miss their own worship time at your church. Most Reform Judaism synagogues welcome other faiths. Send permission forms home for the parents to sign and enlist parents as helpers.

If your community lacks a Jewish synagogue, visit the worship service of another faith tradition.

Prepare

Photocopy the stone tablets (page 72) for each tween.

Provide Bibles, pens, and a piece of wood or cardboard cut to about 9 inches by 12 inches for each tween.

Mix water with glue and provide glue brushes.

Prepare

For each tween provide a simple calendar of the upcoming month as well as stickers of praying hands, Bibles, and crosses.

Prepare

Contact a rabbi in your community and arrange to visit a service at a synagogue.

Provide permission forms and enlist parents as helpers.

Closing Prayer

Thank you, God, that Jesus took time to study and ask questions about God. Thank you for my church, a place where I am welcome to ask questions. Thank you for my church, a place where I can study and grow in my faith. Thank you for my pastor, church leaders, and teachers who help me learn about the Bible and about ways to serve God, Jesus, and others. In Jesus' name we pray. Amen.

Families Can Teach Children Intentional Faith Development

In biblical times, families served as primary educators for their children. Children were taught about God and faith matters in the ebb and flow of family life.

Today families live more fast-paced lives than our biblical ancestors. As a result, families find little time to teach their children about God. They often leave this task up to the church. Yet the church gets small amounts of time to spend with children in religious instruction. Parents share greater quantities of time with children. Parents need to recognize and take seriously their God-ordained role as teachers of the faith.

Churches are important centers for the Intentional Faith Development of children. Yet parents remain the primary educators of children. Congregations help parents fulfill this awesome and sometimes overwhelming task when they partner with families.

Parents who take seriously their role as intentional faith developers for their children commit serious time themselves in studying God's Word and growing in their own faith. Whenever children ask questions they are not competent to answer, these parents readily admit they do not have all of the answers, that they are students along with their children. In humility, they turn to their churches and pastors for help, and when they do, their church does not fail to offer them guidance.

Together congregation and parents work side-by-side in Intentional Faith Development for children. Churches partner with parents because at the baptism of each child, the congregation promises to nurture and support parents. Parents partner with their churches because they recognize the vital role a congregation plays in the life of their children. Both affirm that children are a blessing from God and gifts to both the church and the home.

Suggestions for Ways Families Can Practice Intentional Faith Development

1. Families model Intentional Faith Development for their children by regularly attending Sunday school and other faith development events in the church.
2. Families insist children regularly attend Sunday school and other faith development events designed for children.
3. Parents provide children with their own Bibles appropriate for their ages.
4. Parents show children how to use their Bibles.
5. Parents often read Bible stories to children and discuss these stories.
6. Parents ask their congregations to provide resources for teaching children faith matters at home.
7. Parents avail themselves of opportunities to learn about the Bible.
8. Parents grant themselves opportunities to learn how to teach the Bible to their children.
9. Parents engage children in conversations about Bible stories.
10. Parents answer children's faith questions honestly, but also admit when they do not know answers and seek out help from others.

Stories of Children Practicing Intentional Faith Development

Frazer Memorial United Methodist, Montgomery, Alabama, ministers to special needs children and their families. The church links a special needs child with an adult buddy, allowing parents to attend Sunday school and worship. Katie is one of these special needs children who attend Frazer. Katie is unable to walk or talk. Her grandmother agreed to become her buddy and attend the special needs Sunday school class with Katie. One Sunday, the special needs teacher read the story of Jesus healing the crippled man. When she repeated the words of Jesus found in the story, "Stand up and walk," to everyone's amazement Katie stood up in her wheelchair! The second time the lines were repeated, Katie stood up in her wheelchair. However, at home, Katie refused to stand up no matter how much her family encouraged her. Finally, her grandmother had the idea to reenact the story of Jesus healing the crippled man. Sure enough, as soon as her grandmother said, "Stand up and walk," Katie responded and stood up in her wheelchair. The doctors offer no explanation for her ability to stand up in her wheelchair. Although Katie remains unable to walk, she now stands up as if to proclaim her faith in the healing powers of Jesus! She stands as a witness to the power of effective storytelling and Intentional Faith Development.

At Vestavia Hills United Methodist Church, Birmingham, Alabama, every year children observe the National Day of Prayer by coming together for a prayer breakfast. They eat, share in a prayer activity at the table, listen to a dynamic speaker, and are taught the importance of prayer. The prayer breakfast has impacted the children as they go to school. The children relate that they now start the day off with prayer and silently pray at school before a tough test, about situations with friends, and when they are going through a bad day.

The children's church room at Trenholm Road United Methodist, Columbia, South Carolina, is set up to look like a mini-sanctuary. The children learn all about the worship service by experiencing their own worship time. Each part is taught to them, and as the year progresses, they lead certain parts. Once a month, the children remain in the sanctuary and practice what they have been learning about in children's church. Parents are sent home information about what their children are learning, along with questions parents can ask them. Ideas are given in the take-home materials on ways parents can enhance the worship experiences of their children.

Lily, a precocious four-year-old, attends Frazer Memorial United Methodist in Montgomery, Alabama. As a part of children's worship time, the group of children make power bracelets. On the bracelet, they string different-colored beads to symbolize the salvation story. The lead teacher instructs the children to return back from the craft room to the story room and wait there for their parents to pick them up. However, Lily insists that she needs to wait in the hallway. She keeps telling her teachers, "I need to stand in the hall." The perplexed teachers allow her to stand in the hall under the watchful eye of a helper. This helper observes Lily as she witnesses to everyone who passes by in the hall. She shows them her bracelet and asks them, "Do you have Jesus in your heart?" Several months later, Lily falls into a friend's pool and almost drowns. The doctors sadly inform her family that if she lives she will be brain-dead. Throughout her hospitalization, Lily tightly clutches her power bracelet. Today she is well and continues to wear her power bracelet that enriches her Intentional Faith Development.

First United Methodist, Colorado Springs, Colorado, believes in the power of blessing. They bless each child as they leave Sunday school, they bless babies, they bless children as they finish eating the church fellowship meals, and they bless children as they leave sixth grade to enter the youth group. They bless families of children and bless children's pets.

They use bottles of water and sprinkle them over the heads of children. One preschooler was so captivated by being blessed that he went home and shared with his father. His father was so curious that he inquired about the blessings. This culture of blessing trickled up to the youth and college students, who now desire to receive a blessing from their leaders. Most of these blessings occur as children participate in Intentional Faith Development opportunities. These blessings are intentional, and they teach children that they are blessings from God and gifts to their faith community.

Christ United Methodist, Memphis, Tennessee, offers a BASIC (Brothers and Sisters in Christ) retreat for fourth- and fifth-graders designed to explore faith issues. Eleven-year-old Lane responded to the invitation to accept Christ as his Savior. His parents noticed a dramatic transformation in Lane's life as a result of this decision and due to the impact of the retreat. Lane began studying the book *Welcome to the Family*, which he received at the retreat. His faith impacted his family as he shared with them. His parents committed to devote time reading and studying the Bible as a family and growing their family spiritually as a result of Lane's witness.

Art: Robert S. Jones
© 2002 Cokesbury

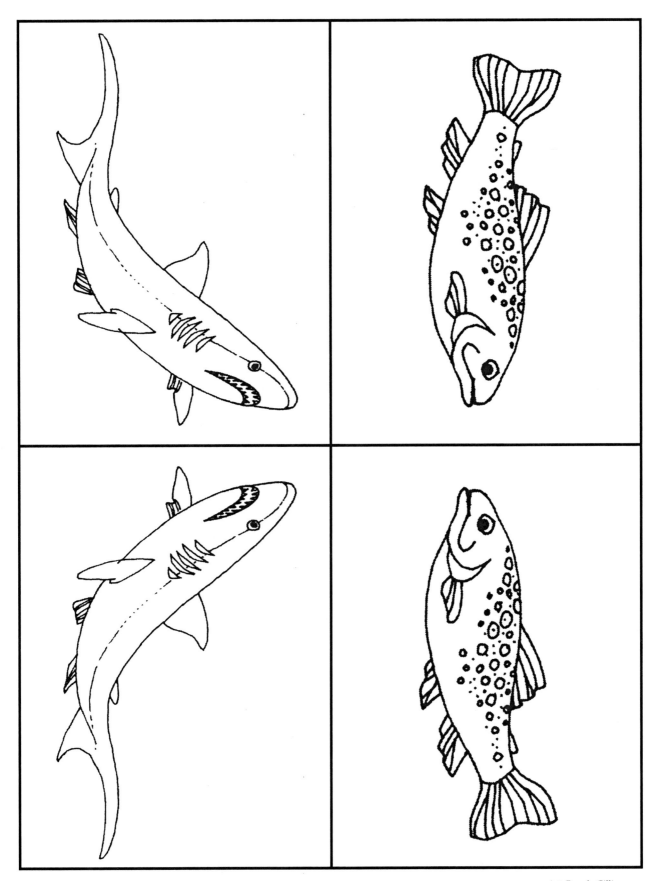

Art: Brenda Gilliam
© 2008 Abingdon Press

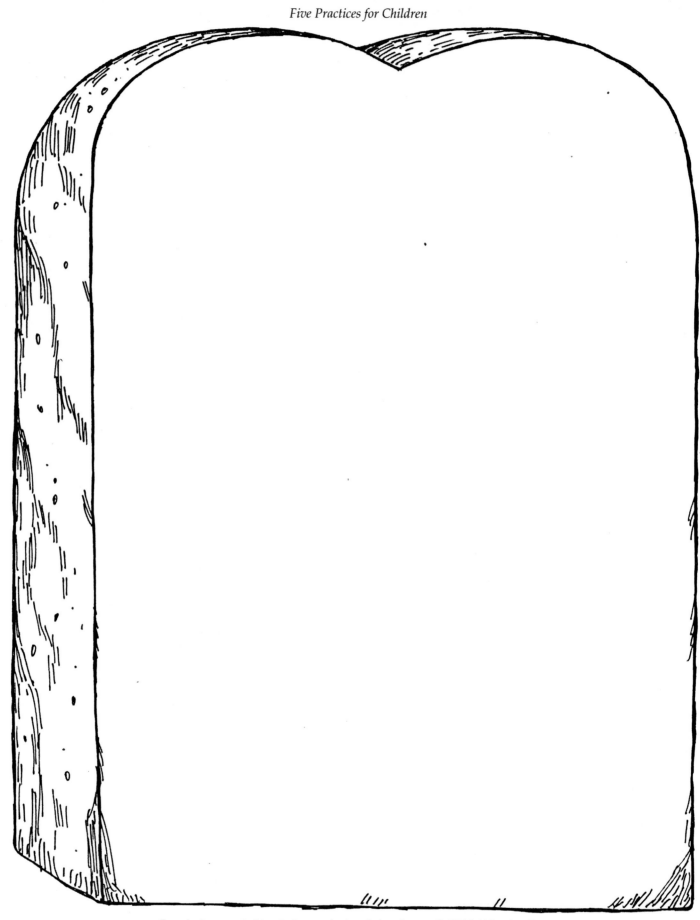

Art: Jim Padgett
© 2006 Cokesbury

4.

Risk-Taking Mission and Service for Children

Introduction

Sixth-grader Lindsey Walker smiles at and welcomes the homeless men and women of her community as she dishes out scrambled eggs. Lindsey serves as a weekly volunteer when her church hosts these visitors for breakfast. This commitment requires her to arise early on Saturday morning when she could be sleeping in, but Lindsey realizes that her service to the community, her church, and her Savior is more important than extra sleep. Her church and her family have taught Lindsey that service to others helps one grow in faith. Each time Lindsey participates, her perspective on homelessness matures, and she comes away from the experience with new understanding of the plight of her homeless friends. Through Risk-Taking Mission and Service, Lindsey serves Christ and her church as a faithful disciple.

Fourth-grader Todd Stephens sorts through the basket of clothes at the local help center in the community located near his church. He carefully places the clothes on hangers so they can be priced and then sold in the help center store. He and his family volunteer monthly at the center. Todd could be spending his time elsewhere, but Todd finds his choice to volunteer at the help center expands his understanding of the Sunday school lessons taught to him about helping others.

Why would a sixth-grader named Lindsey Walker get up early on Saturday morning and spend her time serving meals to the homeless? Why would a fourth-grader named Todd Stephens give up play time with his friends to sort clothes at a community help center? Both of these children engage in Risk-Taking Mission and Service because they have been taught the importance of reaching out to others less fortunate. In Sunday school, teachers instruct Lindsey and Todd in Bible stories about Risk-Taking Mission and Service. In worship, their pastor lifts up Risk-Taking Mission and Service as a means of following Christ more faithfully. Their families teach Lindsey and Todd that "it is more blessed to give than to receive" and then put their words into practice. Lindsey and Todd belong to a congregation that teaches, preaches, and practices Risk-Taking Mission and Service. Lindsey and Todd worship in a faith community that encourages, blesses, and guides children in their efforts to serve.

Lindsey and Todd's endeavors are risk-taking because their experiences move them out of their comfort zones, open their eyes to the needs of others, and help them grow in sensitivity to the struggles of the less fortunate. Lindsey knew little about homelessness when she first volunteered to help serve meals. Now she prays daily for the homeless and calls many of them by name when they enter her church fellowship hall for breakfast. She learns not to look down on those she helps, but to treat them with dignity and respect. Todd realizes that many families have little money to spend for food, clothes, and school supplies for their children. He appreciates his own family's ability to provide adequately for him and his siblings, but he sympathizes with others who struggle to survive. His experience gives him a deeper appreciation and gratitude for his own blessings.

What is Risk-Taking Mission and Service?
What does it have to do with children?

We serve a Savior who models for us Risk-Taking Mission and Service. In Scripture, Christ reaches out to the poor and outcast in his own society and calls us to the same task. Jesus instructs his followers to love our neighbor as ourselves and identifies our neighbor as anyone in need. As a part of our call to radical discipleship, Jesus teaches us to compassionately reach out to those locked in prison, kindly clothe those who are naked, and lovingly feed the hungry.

Risk-Taking Mission and Service propels us out into the world and turns our selfish inward thinking into selfless outward action. Risk-Taking Mission and Service moves us beyond social service to acts of justice and mercy. It opens up our eyes to our own materialistic culture and the simplicity of other cultures and gradually melts away our own feelings of superiority to other nations. Diversity no longer frightens us; rather, it offers us a picture of the kingdom of God. Risk-Taking Mission and Service changes us, matures us, and shapes us into more faithful disciples and prepares us for greater service in God's kingdom.

When a congregation concerns itself only with its own survival and its own internal problems, that congregation lacks vitality and a vision of missions. It faces inward, and members only glimpse service within the walls of the church.

However, when a congregation embraces the challenging call of Christ to reach out beyond the doors of the church and into the world, it comes alive and members get excited. They prepare to step out in faith, grow, change, and risk for the sake of the gospel.

A vibrant church that practices Risk-Taking Mission and Service trains persons before they leave the church, giving them a respectful understanding that mission endeavors are carried out not *to* others but *with* others. They accept the truth that the actual results of Risk-Taking Mission and Service cannot always be measured and that churches may not always know whether their efforts make a difference or not. They also accept the truth that they serve God when they serve others and they come away blessed.

Many churches believe they have done a good job in children's ministry if they create exciting programs and teach creative lessons in the Christian faith. Certainly children need adults to instruct and guide them, but their faith deepens and expands when they are allowed to put their faith into practice through service to others. Most children enjoy mission projects and delight in serving others. Risk-Taking Mission and Service allows them to encounter persons different from them and learn to love and respect these individuals. Risk-Taking Mission and Service takes children from their own familiar surroundings into a different culture or social environment. It transforms sheltered children into compassionate children.

Obviously children need training before they engage in Risk-Taking Mission and Service. Adult leaders must inform children of what they may encounter, alleviate any fears, and work alongside them. Adults leaders become effective mentors for children when they exhibit patience, answer questions honestly, and understand the initial reluctance of some children to fully engage themselves. Churches that involve children should also recruit families so that children find comfort and safety in the shared interest of family members. A family working together relieves much of the stress and uncertainty children bring with them. Congregations must never engage children in any mission or service project without the consent and approval of parents or guardians.

God calls children as well as adults into service. In the Old Testament, the young boy Samuel helps the priest Eli in the Temple. The risky part of his service entails recognizing the call of God, heeding that call, and preparing to speak prophetic words against the injustices of the religious leaders of his time. God blesses Samuel with a strong mentor who affirms God's call.

Today God continues to call children to service.

God calls the reluctant young Jeremiah and promises to give him the words to speak. The risky part of his service comes when he reluctantly accepts God's call, faithfully prepares himself to follow God's instructions, and unwaveringly agrees to speak harsh, prophetic words that will upset his hearers.

Miriam helps her mother hide her brother Moses in the bulrushes. When the Pharaoh's daughter discovers Moses, Miriam boldly suggests a nursemaid from the Jewish people. She secures her own mother for the job. Miriam's actions allow her family to care for Moses until the time he is weaned and goes to live at the court. Miriam partners with her mother in a risky plan to save Moses, a daring move that ultimately secures the liberation of the children of Israel from bondage in Egypt.

Young David volunteers for a risk-taking mission to fight the giant Goliath. His courage shows his confidence in God and saves the nation of Israel from further ridicule by the Philistines. David draws his strength from God rather than relying on military might.

Today God continues to call children to service. God endows the children in our churches with wonderful and abundant gifts. We do our children a disservice when we fail to affirm their calls to Risk-Taking Mission and Service.

Like Eli, we must help children examine their call and then take the necessary steps to help them fulfill that call through chances to practice Risk-Taking Mission and Service. We do so with the assurance and confidence that, like Jeremiah, God forms each of them in the womb, knows each before birth, and consecrates them for worthy and useful service.

Workshop for Lesson Four

Encourage the members of your children's ministry team, your Sunday school teachers, and other volunteers in your children's ministry area to gather for a time of teaching and reflection on the ways children in your church may be involved in acts of Risk-Taking Mission and Service.

Prayer and Welcome

Reflections on 1 Samuel 17:19-50

Since this is a long Scripture passage, divide into four teams to read and discuss the Scripture passage, then return as a group to share insights.

Team One: Read 1 Samuel 17:19-23. Discuss the following questions.
1. Why was David in the camp of the Israelite soldiers? (Read 1 Samuel 17:17-18.)
2. How do you think David felt when he heard the jeering words of the giant Goliath?
3. Read 1 Samuel 17:4-7 and write a description of the giant Goliath.

Team Two: Read 1 Samuel 17:24-30. Discuss the following questions.
1. What rewards did Saul promise the man who killed Goliath?
2. Why was David's older brother upset with him?
3. How many brothers did David have? What was the name of David's father? What were the names of the brothers who were fighting? (Read 1 Samuel 17:12-16.)

Team Three: Read 1 Samuel 17:31-40.
1. Why was Saul reluctant to allow David to fight Goliath?
2. How did David persuade Saul he could fight?
3. Draw a picture of the clothing Saul put on David for the battle.

Team Four: Read 1 Samuel 17:41-50.
1. How does David justify his actions in fighting Goliath?
2. Read the United Methodist stand on war in the *Book of Discipline*. Have team members discuss this stand.
3. Reflect on how teachers might teach this passage in light of the vivid details of war and killing found in the passage.

List on a board or flip chart all of the ways David engaged in a risk-taking mission.

Some examples might be:
1. He was only a boy.
2. He took a risk when he suggested his idea to King Saul, who could have become very angry, especially given Saul's mental state.

3. He risked the anger and jealousy of his brothers and other soldiers, as he was only a shepherd and not a trained warrior.
4. He risked his life.

Affirm the Ways Your Children Now Engage in Risk-Taking Mission and Service

Take time to explain why certain mission and service projects would be considered risk-taking and others, though good, do not involve risk. An example might be your recent vacation Bible school project. Here are two different scenarios.

Scenario One: Your children collect items or money for a good cause, but this endeavor does not involve any risk on the part of the children in terms of leaving their comfort zones. They bring money and supplies and learn about their mission project, but they do not deliver the money/supplies or talk with those whom the project is intended to help.

Scenario Two: Not only do your children collect money and supplies for a worthy cause, but you also allow the children to deliver the money/supplies and tour the facility you help. The children meet and talk with some persons whose lives are impacted by the work of the facility. They spend some time volunteering at this facility.

Reproduce copies of the "Risk-Taking Mission and Service Checklist" on page 95 and hand them out. On the left-hand side participants are to list all the ways children in your church practice mission and service either in the present or in the recent past. In the middle section they are to indicate if the experience was risk-taking and why. If participants did not consider the mission/service endeavor risk-taking, have them offer suggestions on the right-hand side of the chart for ways to improve the project for the children so that it becomes a Risk-Taking Mission and Service experience. (Two examples have been filled in.)

If time permits, invite a child in your church who regularly practices Risk-Taking Mission and Service to come and talk about the experience.

Where to Go From Here?

Share the teaching materials in this chapter that are designed for a Sunday school lesson, children's worship lesson, or special teaching session. There are teaching materials for separate use with preschool, elementary, and older elementary (tween) children. Decide as a group how and when you will teach this material to the children. Set a date for the teaching of these lessons. After the lessons are taught, determine how you will use the ideas for Risk-Taking Mission and Service that the children have chosen. For example, you might designate a preschool teacher who will share the ideas of the younger children, but you will want to invite representative elementary and older children to share the ideas of their age groups.

Celebrate and Affirm the Ideas of Children

Hold a mission fair for the children. Invite parents to attend as well. Gather materials from local missions in your community or city. If your church participates in the Meals on Wheels program, invite someone to come who works with the program in your church. If your church reaches out to persons in other countries, provide a map of each country and pictures if available. Set up card tables and display the items, pictures, and information. You will want to show the children ways the church currently serves others as well as new ideas for mission projects. Give the children time to visit each center. Have an adult present in each center to talk with the children. Give children a notebook and pencil when they arrive. Let elementary children and tweens write down some things they learn or observe in the centers. Preschool children may wish to draw pictures.

Serve sandwiches, chips, fruit, cookies, and juice.

After lunch, gather the children and let them share what they observed at the mission fair. Ask a child who is already involved in risk-taking mission to share. Explain to the children the difference between Risk-Taking Mission and Service and other projects in your church. Provide them examples of ideas for Risk-Taking Mission and Service.

For example, you might say, "Our church collects canned goods each month for our local community help center. Our risk-taking mission project could involve collecting these canned goods. We could travel to the help center one Saturday a month and sort the food. We might even be able to help give the food to people when they visit the help center. We can call the director and find out what she or he needs us to do."

Or you might say, "Our church provides a meal for homeless men in our community once a week. Different people in our church volunteer to cook the meal. You could host this meal for the homeless men. Your families will prepare the meal; you will serve the meal and sing for the men. We can make placemats in our classes and put together gift bags for the men. We can also make them a lunch to carry with them when they leave."

Let the children talk about this in small groups. Come back and see if one project seems to interest the majority of the children. Guide children in the necessary steps to carry out the mission project.

Two Examples of Risk-Taking Mission and Service:

Your children have chosen to collect canned goods for a local mission and volunteer at the mission once a month.
1. Gain the support of your pastor, staff, and church leaders.
2. Talk with the director of the mission and invite him or her to come and speak with the children in a joint gathering of the Sunday school classes.
3. Hold a meeting of parents to explain the project.
4. Have one child speak in worship asking members to collect canned goods and bring them to the church once a month.
5. Have children decorate boxes to hold the canned goods, and put the boxes in strategic places around the church. Place a box in every adult Sunday school class.
6. Have children speak in adult Sunday school classes and ask members to reserve one Sunday each month to bring canned goods. Choose the Sunday prior to the Saturday the children are to work at the mission so you have canned goods to take with you.
7. Have children draw "advertisements" on paper asking for monthly donations of canned goods and distribute copies in every Sunday school class.
8. Have children write newsletter articles.
9. Develop a sign-up sheet for one year. Determine how many children and adults are needed for your monthly trip to the mission. Let children and adults sign up for the month they are willing to serve. Send reminder notices.
10. Let children write newsletter articles after their volunteer work is complete, sharing with church members what they did and how the experience impacted their lives.

Your children have chosen to collect and distribute coats, hats, gloves, scarves, and socks for the homeless in your community.
1. Gain the support of your pastor, staff, and church leaders.
2. Have several children speak in your worship service about this vision of the children.
3. Have one child or several children write newsletter articles.
4. Have children make posters.
5. Have children research the needs of the homeless in your community. Ask them to interview persons who work with the homeless and share this information with the congregation through the newsletter.
6. Select the months of September and October to gather the coats, depending on your seasonal changes. You will want to distribute the coats before winter weather sets in.
7. Have children decorate boxes for the items and put the boxes in various locations throughout your church building. Have church members leave the items in these boxes.
8. Contact an agency that works with the homeless to ensure greater safety for the children and church members. The contact person should offer the children insight into the homeless. Be sure that adults are recruited who will assist the children.
9. Deliver the items to the homeless with the instructions and help of your contact person at the mission or community agency.
10. Provide a time for the children to share their experiences and let them decide if they wish to make this a yearly mission outreach project of your church.

A Child Practices Risk-Taking Mission and Service

Objective:

The children will:
- Hear 1 Samuel 17:19-50.
- Learn the story of David and how he volunteers for a risk-taking mission to fight the giant Goliath and loyally serves his nation of Israel.
- Learn ways children can engage in Risk-Taking Mission and Service.

Bible Story:

1 Samuel 17:19-50: Risk-taking David volunteers for a daring mission and fights the giant Goliath.

Bible Verse:

David said to the Philistine, "You come at me with sword and spear and javelin; but I come to you in the name of the Lord of hosts."
                    1 Samuel 17:45, NRSV

Focus for the Teacher

One of the favorite Bible stories of children remains the story of David and Goliath. This story intrigues children due to its vivid action and its depiction of child heroics. After all, the hero of the story turns out to be a child! The Scripture fails to give us David's exact age, but he was apparently too young to serve in the Israelite army. In our story, taken from 1 Samuel 17, the armies of the Philistines and the army of Israel face each other for battle, camped out on opposite sides of a valley. Day after day, a nine-foot giant named Goliath continues to taunt the Israelite army and no one dares stop his jeering remarks out of fear. David steps into the picture when he arrives to bring supplies to

his older brothers who serve in the army. David bravely volunteers to fight the giant, but it takes some persuasion before King Saul allows David to enter the battle. David convinces Saul that, as a keeper of sheep, he fights bears and lions when they try to attack his sheep. David regards Goliath as one of these wild beasts.

The Israelites believe God sanctions and blesses their military operations. The army functions as the army of the Lord. Thus, when Goliath criticizes the army, he also ridicules their God, the true commander of the army. This concept of war helps us to better understand David's passionate desire to defend the honor and integrity of his nation against Goliath.

One cannot help laughing at the scene where Saul outfits young David with his own armor, sword, and helmet. Can you imagine how ridiculous the young boy looked as he struggled to walk? David resorts to the familiar, taking his staff, five smooth stones, his slingshot, and his shepherd's pouch. David returns to his true identity as shepherd boy. He cannot fight the giant by pretending to be who he is not. David uses the gifts God gives him and the tools of his shepherd trade to outsmart the giant Goliath.

David volunteers for his Risk-Taking Mission and Service to his country out of his love for his nation and his God. No one asks David to get involved. In fact, David's older brother Eliab chastises David after he discovers David talking with the soldiers rather than tending his sheep. One might argue that David wants the rewards King Saul offers: his eldest daughter in marriage and freedom for the family. These enticements may play a part in David's decision, but they should not erase David's risk-taking courage. Trained soldiers in the army hear of the rewards and, out of fear, take no action. Only young David steps forward, so we are justified in commending him for his bravery.

The biblical writer confuses us when in chapter 17 Saul appears not to know David, although the previous chapter highlights David's role as the king's musician and armor-bearer (16:14-23). We find difficulty in reconciling the two images of David's rela-

The story teaches us to depend on God when we face giants in our lives.

tionship to Saul. It helps us to remember that biblical writers do not always place events in chronological order in the text. Scholars offer several reasonable explanations. One recalls that Saul suffers from a mental illness ("evil spirit"), and this malady might prevent Saul from recognizing David. Some writers reason that enough time elapses between David's service at the court and the current scene that David's appearance changes significantly. Others think Saul pretends not to know David out of jealousy.

Some teachers find it hard to teach this story due to their opposition to war. Sharing the facts of the biblical story should not compromise this stand. Most children accept the reality of war, and the story of heroic David captures their attention rather than the moral dilemma that challenges some adult readers. Be aware that older children could argue about the validity of war, especially if they come from families that oppose war. Read our United Methodist stand on war stated in our *Book of Discipline* in case children present you with difficult questions.

The heart of this story centers on the risk-taking actions of a young boy who takes a stand for what he believes and fights for the honor of his nation. His daring mission saves the integrity of his people and prevents their total humiliation. The story teaches us to depend on God when we face giants in our lives, those huge fearful situations that threaten our faith. We highlight the risk-taking efforts of a young boy who trusts in God so that when children face their own giants they, too, turn to the God whom David loves and defends.

Preschool

Risk-Taking Mission and Service

Welcome the Children to Risk-Taking Mission and Service

Welcome the children by name. Ask the children to go over to the mural paper. Have each child stand with his or her back to the paper. Use a yardstick or tape measure to measure the child. Record the height of the child and write his or her name beside the height on the paper.

Tell the children that their Bible story for today is about a young boy and a man who was very tall. He was nine feet tall!

Have the children color the story picture (page 96). Point out David in the picture and Goliath in the picture.

Share the Bible Story (1 Samuel 17:19-50)

Place a small amount of water in the swimming pool and put plants around it to suggest a brook. **(Caution: Never leave the water unattended.)** Put enough pebbles in the water for each child to take five pebbles.

Gather the children around the brook. Tell them the story of David and Goliath using a children's storybook or children's Bible or have a storyteller dressed as David tell the story to the children.

Reinforce the Story

Let each child take five stones from the brook. Count with the children as they remove the stones from the brook. Provide towels so the children can dry their stones. Have the children take their stones to a table and sit down.

Prepare

Mount four feet of mural paper on the wall.

Provide a yardstick or tape measure and crayons or markers.

Photocopy the David and Goliath picture (page 96) for each child.

Prepare

Purchase or borrow a plastic swimming pool or large tub.

Provide pebbles and plants. You will need five pebbles for each child.

Provide a children's Bible or Bible storybook or recruit someone to wear a Bible-times costume and tell the story.

Give each child a small cloth sack or paper bag. Have the children place their stones inside the sack and help them tie the sack securely.

Teach the children motions they are to use as you share again the story of David and Goliath. When they hear the name "Goliath" they are to put one hand as high up in the air as they can to indicate how tall Goliath stood.

When they hear the name "David" they are to hold up their bags with the stones inside and shake them.

When you count the stones in the story, they are to hold up the correct number of fingers on their hands as you say each number. Practice holding up one finger, then two fingers, and so on until the children can hold up five fingers.

David *(shake bag)* was a young boy who took care of his father's sheep. He was a good shepherd. When wolves, bears, or lions came near the sheep, David *(shake bag)* chased them away. David played music for the sheep, and this helped them go to sleep. One day a man named Goliath *(put hand up high)* wanted to hurt David *(shake bag)* and his friends. The king needed some help fighting Goliath because he was nine feet tall. Everyone was afraid of Goliath *(put hand up high)* and no one would fight him. David *(shake bag)* went to a small brook and got one *(put up one finger)*, two *(put up two fingers)*, three *(put up three fingers)*, four *(put up four fingers)*, five *(put up five fingers)* stones from the brook. He put one in his slingshot, he threw the stone, and Goliath *(put hand up high)* fell to the ground. Even though David *(shake bag)* was not as tall as Goliath *(put hand up high)*, he was a brave boy and helped save his friends from danger.

David the Shepherd Pictures

Provide simple costumes so the children can dress up as David. Take a piece of cloth, cut a hole in the top for the child's head, and put it over the child like a poncho. Tie a sash around the waist. Put on a headpiece. Construct a shepherd's staff out of heavy cardboard.

Encourage each child to stand by the height measurement chart and find his or her name. Explain to the children that David was not as tall as Goliath, but God needed David as a helper. Tell the children that God needs each child no matter what height they are.

Prepare

Use the pool and pebbles arranged earlier.

Provide paper towels and a small pouch or paper bag for each child.

Pouches may be purchased online at www.oriental-trading.com.

Prepare

Provide Bible-times costumes.

Make a shepherd's staff from cardboard.

Provide a camera.

Take a picture of each child holding the shepherd's staff. If you have a large class you may wish to construct more than one staff to make the picture-taking time shorter. Once the pictures are ready, give them to the children as a reminder of the lesson.

Play a Bible Game

Have a teacher or assistant play the role of King Saul. Place a crown on this person's head. Have the children sit in a circle. Show the children the stuffed-animal sheep. Remind the children that David took care of sheep.

Play music and have the children pass the sheep around the circle. Stop the music and have King Saul ask the child with the sheep, by name, if he or she will help him. The child goes and stands behind King Saul. Continue to play the game until all the children are standing behind King Saul. The last child left in the circle goes to the front of the line as David and all of the children clap for him. He and King Saul lead the group to snack time.

Snack Time

As the children eat their snacks talk with them about the ways David helped King Saul and his friends. Suggest to the children that they can help others.

Practice Risk-Taking Mission and Service

Encourage the children to decorate the covered box with crayons or markers. Tell the children to bring canned goods to put in the box. Send notes home with the children asking parents to allow children to bring canned goods. Select a place where the box will be located.

Plan a class trip so that children and their families can deliver the canned goods to a community center that distributes to the needy. Let the children visit the center. Or select a family in the community that needs the canned goods and have the children and their families deliver the canned goods to that family.

Closing Prayer

Thank you, God, that David was a helper. Thank you that David was brave. I want to be brave. I want to help others like David. Amen.

Prepare

Provide a crown, a stuffed-animal sheep, a CD of preschool praise music, and a CD player.

Prepare

Provide simple snacks, juice, napkins, and cups.

Prepare

Cover a large box with plain paper.

Provide crayons or markers.

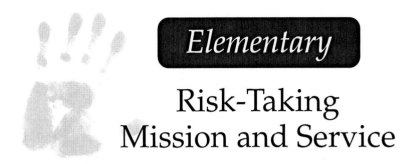

Risk-Taking Mission and Service

Welcome the Children to Risk-Taking Mission and Service

Welcome each child by name. As each child arrives, have him or her go over to the heart box or bag and pick out a picture card. Each card shows an object. Have the child take the card to a table and draw a picture of how someone could use the object to help people. For example, a hammer could be used to build a Habitat for Humanity house. Tell the children that today's lesson deals with the way we share God's love with others and do so in a big, huge way that changes us. Let the children share their drawings.

Prepare

Photocopy and cut apart the object cards (page 97).

Decorate a box or bag with hearts and put the cards inside.

Provide paper and pencils.

Share the Bible Story (1 Samuel 17:19-50)

Gather the children and have them sit on a rug. Ask the children to listen very carefully as they are to play a Bible game after the story. Tell them the Bible story using a children's Bible or Bible storybook. Be sure to include the answers to the Bible game questions in the story.

Prepare

Provide a children's Bible or Bible storybook.

Play a Bible Game

Divide the children into two teams. Ask the questions below, alternating between teams. Have the children on each team take turns. When a question is answered correctly, the team receives a small pebble. If the question is answered incorrectly, the team loses a turn. The winning team is the one that collects the most pebbles by the end of the game.

Prepare

Provide ten pebbles.

1. What was the name of the king in our story? *(King Saul)*
2. How many brothers did David have? *(seven)*
3. What was the name of David's father? *(Jesse)*
4. Who were the Jewish people fighting against? *(Philistines)*
5. What was the name of the giant? *(Goliath)*
6. How tall was Goliath? *(nine feet tall)*

7. What was David's job at home? *(taking care of his father's sheep)*
8. Why was David at the battlefield? *(He was bringing food and supplies to his older brothers.)*
9. What items did Saul place on David? *(armor, sword, helmet)*
10. What did David use to fight Goliath? *(slingshot and five smooth stones)*

Teach the Children About Risk-Taking Mission and Service

Prepare

Invite a missionary, former missionary, community leader, or mission leader in your church to speak with the children.

If you invite a missionary or former missionary, ask him or her to bring items from the country he or she served to show the children. Ask this person to share some stories of risk-taking in service to God.

If you invite a community leader, ask him or her to share ways in which volunteers change or grow as a result of their volunteer efforts.

If you invite a mission leader, ask him or her to share ways in which church members change and grow as they participate in service projects.

When the guest leaves, explain to the children that there are many nice things we do in the church, such as collecting items or sending money, that do not require us to get involved in meeting the people we are helping. Risk-Taking Mission and Service helps us meet people and learn from them.

Name some mission projects your church sponsors or participates in. Ask the children to raise their hands after you name a project if they believe it fits the category of risk-taking. Remind the children that Risk-Taking Mission and Service gets persons involved.

Here are some examples:
1. Collecting money to send to Africa.
2. Sorting clothes at the local help center. *(raise hands)*
3. Collecting shoes for Soles for Souls.
4. Feeding people at the homeless center. *(raise hands)*
5. Cooking a meal for the homeless and serving them. *(raise hands)*
6. Collecting pennies to buy Bibles for persons in Russia.
7. Taking Christmas presents to the home of a needy family. *(raise hands)*
8. The children's choir singing at a nursing home and talking with the elderly. *(raise hands)*

9. A child's family inviting a lonely, older person to eat Thanksgiving dinner with them. *(raise hands)*
10. Making cards for the homebound and mailing them.
11. Making cards for the homebound and delivering them in person. *(raise hands)*
12. Collecting pet supplies and food for the local animal shelter.
13. Volunteering time at the animal shelter. *(raise hands)*
14. Inviting other children in the community to attend vacation Bible school. *(raise hands)*
15. Collecting school supplies for needy children.

Explain to the children that all of these projects are good, but some of them help us meet the people being helped and understand their circumstances.

Practice Risk-Taking Mission and Service

Offer suggestions to the children on ways they can practice Risk-Taking Mission and Service in their community. Select a class mission project. Let the children plan ways to collect necessary items for the mission endeavor and carry it out as a class.

Talk with the pastor and secure his or her support. If the children plan to collect items and take them to a center, talk with the director. If the children plan to volunteer services at a community agency, secure the permission of the parents and invite families to attend. Talk with the director of the agency. If the children wish to reach out to needy families or children in the community, secure names from a local agency and seek the advice of the director.

Educate the children, collect the items as needed, and carry out the mission project. Have children talk about their experiences of meeting new people and how the experiences changed them.

Snack Time With David

As the children eat their snack, have a youth dressed as David the shepherd boy enter the classroom. Have him talk about his experiences as a shepherd boy and about the risky time in his life when he had to fight the giant Goliath. Let him give each child five smooth stones to take with them.

Stepping Stones to Risky Mission

Prepare

Cut out large stones from butcher paper and tape these to the floor in a circle. Have one stone that looks completely different from the other stones.

Provide a crown, a CD of praise music, and a CD player.

Point out the different stone to the children. Have the children stand on one stone. Play music and have the children move in a forward circle around the stones.

Stop the music and direct them to stop on a stone. The child who lands on the stone that looks different gets crowned as King Saul. Place a crown on his or her head. He or she picks one child to be David. The child selected as David moves from the stone he or she is standing on and joins King Saul on his stone. Together, they walk on the same stones as the music starts again.

The next child who lands on the special stone gets to wear the crown of King Saul, and he or she picks a child to be David. They walk on the same stones as the music starts again. Play this game several times to remind the children that David helped King Saul.

Closing Prayer

Thank you, God, for David and the way he helped the King. I want to help others in the same daring and risky way David did. Amen.

Risk-Taking Mission and Service

Welcome the Children to Risk-Taking Mission and Service

Prepare

Before the class session, purchase decorative stones at a hobby store, craft store, or home supply store.

Welcome the children by name. Give each child a large decorative stone. Explain to the children as they arrive that the Bible story for their class time is the story of David and Goliath. David faces a giant in his life, and the children also face giants in their lives.

Provide markers and ask the children to write their names on one side of the stone. On the other side ask them to write a giant problem in their life. Ask the children to take their stones and place them around the base of a cross. Be sure their names are facing up.

Place a cross in the room and provide markers.

Bible Study (1 Samuel 17:19-50)

Prepare

Have tweens read the Bible story from 1 Samuel 17:19-50. Some children may have questions about war. Share with them the United Methodist perspective on war stated in *The Book of Discipline*. Give time for the children to share their opinions.

Familiarize yourself with the Book of Discipline's *section on war.*

Provide Bibles.

Reinforce the Bible Study

Prepare

Divide the following assignments among your tweens:

Provide paper and pencils.

1. Select five tweens. Ask them to write an editorial newspaper article on one of the following events.
   A. King Saul's perspective on Goliath.
   B. King Saul's perspective on David.
   C. David's perspective on fighting Goliath.
   D. Goliath's perspective on David.
   E. David's older brother's perspective on King Saul allowing David to fight Goliath.

2. Ask one tween to write a letter from David to Saul describing why he is qualified to fight Goliath.
3. Ask one tween to write an advertisement describing the attributes of Goliath.
4. Ask one tween to write an advertisement from King Saul urging someone to come forward to fight Goliath and listing the rewards he will offer.
5. Ask one tween to write a newspaper article describing David's day as a shepherd boy.
6. Ask one tween to write a prayer from David to God.

If you have more children in the class than parts, repeat some of the assignments. Let the children who are willing share their writings.

Understanding Risk-Taking Service

Divide the class into three groups.
1. Have group one look up the phrase *risk-taking* in the dictionary or on the computer. Ask the group to answer this question: How was David's mission risky?
2. Have group two look up the word *mission* in the dictionary or on the computer. Ask the group to answer this question: How was David's contest with Goliath a mission for him?
3. Have group three look up the word *service* in the dictionary or on the computer. Ask the group to answer this question: How did David provide service for the king and his nation?

Come back together as a group and share your findings.

Exploring Risk-Taking Mission and Service in Your Church

Tell the children that you are sending them on an important mission adventure as detectives. Divide the children into groups of three or four. Secure a youth or an adult volunteer to go with each group. Give the children small notebooks and pens to record their findings. Ask the children to snoop out ways their church involves itself in mission and service. Tell the children to write down whether they think the mission project is risk-taking or not and why. Send the children out on their mission adventure. Here are some things to look for:
1. Bulletin boards that highlight mission work the church supports.
2. Bulletin boards that highlight mission work in other countries.

Prepare

Provide computers or dictionaries.

Prepare

Recruit youth or adult helpers as needed.

Provide small notebooks, pens, stickers, newsprint, and markers.

3. Boxes or containers shattered around the church for special mission collections.
4. The pastor or other staff members who can give short interviews to provide ideas.
5. Any current mission projects of the children.

When the tweens return to class, list all of the mission projects on newsprint. Give the tweens a package of stickers. Then ask each tween to come up and place a sticker beside each mission project he or she considers risk-taking. See which projects gain the most stickers. Talk with the tweens about why they selected certain projects and not others.

Practice Risk-Taking Mission and Service

Allow tweens to brainstorm about a Risk-Taking Mission and Service project for the class. Be sure that the project the tweens select allows them to interact with the persons they seek to serve and offers them opportunities to grow in their perspectives. Plan the event and secure approval of the pastor, family members, and the leader of any community agency that is involved. Select a date and carry out the mission project. Have the tweens gather and share the impact of the mission project in their lives.

Risk-Taking Mission and Service Commitment Card for Families

Give the tweens the Risk-Taking Mission and Service commitment card (see page 98). Encourage the tweens to put off filling out the card until they share together in the class risk-taking mission project, as some may want to make this project their future commitment on a regular basis.

Have the tweens discuss with their families a weekly, monthly, or quarterly Risk-Taking Mission and Service project that the family can share together. Pray about the project. Gather information and talk with directors of the agency the family wishes to help.

Closing Prayer

Thank you, God, for brave and risk-taking David. Help me to turn to you when I have giants to fight in my own life. Help me to find ways to practice Risk-Taking Mission and Service. In Jesus' name we pray. Amen.

Prepare

Photocopy the commitment card on page 98 for each tween.

Families Can Teach Children Risk-Taking Mission and Service

Practices of Risk-Taking Mission and Service in family life prepare children for a lifetime of discipleship. When children interact with their families in serving others, they remember the experiences and carry them with them into youth and adulthood. They are more likely to continue practices of Risk-Taking Mission and Service when their families teach them at a young age how to care and to serve others. They fondly remember family shared mission projects that impact their lives, change their perspective, and force them out of their comfort zone to confront the needs of others. Children find comfort and security when their families work alongside them.

From the response of their families to others less fortunate, children learn how to respect and love all of God's children. When families share together in Risk-Taking Mission and Service, they grow closer, practice their faith, and risk for the sake of others.

Families have the responsibility to model for and teach children Christ-like attitudes and actions toward strangers and the marginalized of society. What better way to teach and show Christian love than to practice Risk-Taking Mission and Service as a family and to do so in a kind, compassionate, Christ-like manner?

Suggestions for Ways Families Can Practice Risk-Taking Mission and Service

1. Support your congregation's efforts at Risk-Taking Mission and Service and educate your children about projects of your church family.
2. Select a Risk-Taking Mission and Service project of your church and work together as a family. Commit to and devote a certain amount of time per week, per month, or per quarter as your family schedule allows.
3. Volunteer time as a family at a homeless shelter, animal shelter, or community outreach program.
4. Clean out your garage, attic, closets, and toy boxes and give unused items to a local community program that helps individuals in need. Take the items as a family and volunteer your help.
5. Share your Thanksgiving dinner with someone who is lonely or in need.
6. Volunteer to serve lunch to the homeless on Thanksgiving. Contact the Salvation Army or your local rescue mission.
7. Reach out to a needy family at Christmas. Purchase and wrap presents, then deliver them as a family and spend some time getting to know the family you are helping.
8. Participate in the Locks of Love program. Children participate by volunteering to cut their hair when it reaches a certain length so wigs can be made for cancer patients.
9. Help and support your child's decision to plan a birthday party for himself or herself at which instead of bringing gifts, other children bring donations of money or designated items to help the needy.

Stories of Children Practicing Risk-Taking Mission and Service

For twenty years, during the week of vacation Bible school, the fourth- and fifth-graders of Haymount United Methodist in Fayetteville, North Carolina, have gone out into the community instead of staying at church to hear Bible stories, play games, and make crafts. The KidServe program gives the children a venue to practice risk-taking ministry by putting them into situations that are unfamiliar to them and, at times, uncomfortable for them.

Over the years the children have gone gleaning for a large variety of crops and then brought them to the distribution centers in the community; they have played games and shared stories with disabled veterans in the VA Hospital; they have sorted clothing at the Urban Ministries in the community, they have sorted food at the local food bank, they have cleaned out kennels and walked homeless pets—the list goes on and on.

The children are learning by doing acts of Risk-Taking Mission and Service. They are also learning the essential lesson that giving of oneself in Risk-Taking Mission and Service is the culminating part of the Great Commandment—Love God and love your neighbor.

In the summer of 2010, First United Methodist, Jonesboro, Arkansas, committed a week in Buras, Louisiana, at Trinity United Methodist to fellowship and to lift up the spirits of the fishing community. The fishing industry of Louisiana suffered immensely from the explosion of the Deepwater Horizon oil rig in the Gulf of Mexico on April 20, 2010. In addition, this community was still in need of repair physically, spiritually, and emotionally since Hurricane Katrina in 2005. The mission team worked around the church, painting rooms, planting flowers and shrubs, repairing swings, and building bookcases.

It was not long before the children of Arkansas found common ground with the children of Buras. The church hosted a vacation Bible school and the children of both communities enjoyed singing popular songs together, splashing around in water, and breaking bread over gumbo. In separate interviews, all the children said they got more out of the trip than they gave. Every child commented on how the people of Buras love endlessly. A boy named Austin added, "They are very appreciative and they don't take things for granted."

Each child was asked what he or she took away from this mission experience. Maddie said, "One thing that I learned is that being a Christian is hard and these people still love and worship God, even though they have had hard times, because they put Jesus first."

Two Christmases ago, the fourth- and fifth-graders of Frazer United Methodist Church in Montgomery, Alabama, studied about the importance of service to others. One of the adult leaders talked with the class about an experience of Risk-Taking Mission and Service carried out by one of his friends, who happened to attend the church. His friend, driving his car on a bitterly cold night, saw a man and woman in wheelchairs with a child perched on each of their laps. The friend stopped and talked with the couple. He found out that the wheelchairs were their only mode of transportation, so he worked to get them motorized wheelchairs.

This story of Risk-Taking Mission and Service so impacted quiet Jodie that she went home and insisted that more action needed to be taken to help this family whose parents were wheelchair-bound. Through her efforts, Jodie secured the help of adults who aided the family in securing a home without any cost to them. Jodie visited with the family several times and helped her family plan and host a picnic for the family. Jodie's mother was active in the church, but not her father. Jodie's loving outreach actions affected her father, and he has since accepted Christ as his Savior and regularly worships at Frazer.

Aldersgate United Methodist, North Reading, Massachusetts, leads annual mission trips to Maine. They help migrant workers and assist Neighbors Helping Neighbors, a construction ministry to the local poor. The children on the mission trip work hard hauling wood scraps, painting, nailing down roofing shingles, and more. Children make friends easily with the home occupants, their children, and pets, ministering through friendship. The children sort clothing and shoes as part of a clothing ministry targeted toward migrant blueberry rakers and the local poor.

When the children of Aldersgate United Methodist return home and are asked by others, "What did you do on your summer vacation?" the account of their trip turns into a witness. Formed and shaped by their experience, children act as salt and light simply by telling the story of the fun they had and the work they accomplished.

Risk-Taking Mission and Service Checklist

Mission/Service Project	Risk-Taking and Why	How to Improve
Collected coats for the homeless	Yes—We had children deliver. They talked with homeless.	
VBS project for local help center food drive	No—All we did was collect.	We could have taken the children to the center and let them shelve the food and help distribute it to the clients.

Art: Benton Mahan
© 2007 Cokesbury

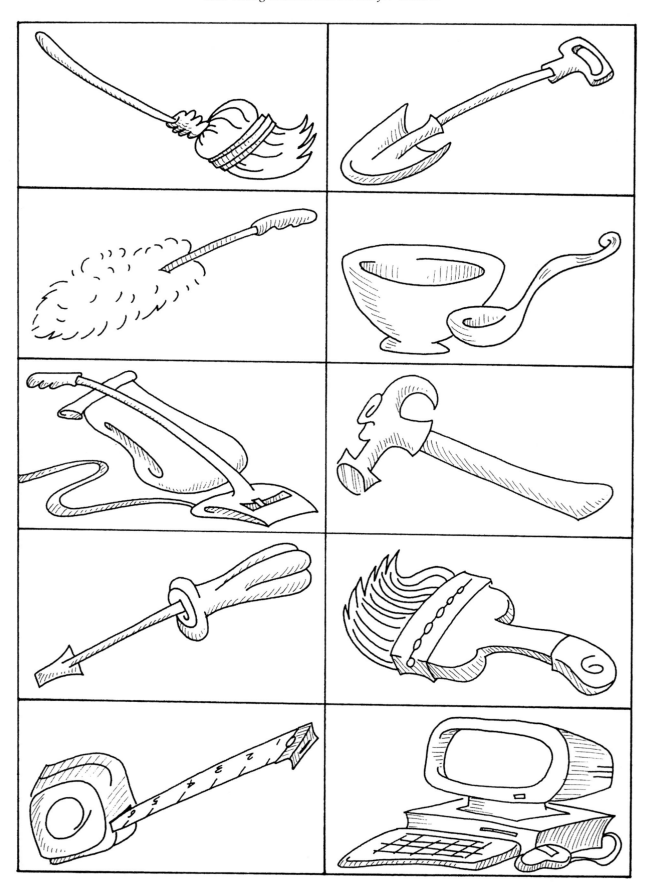

Art: Megan Jeffery
© 1998 Abingdon Press

We, the

_____family,

pledge to serve

__weekly, __monthly, __quarterly

at _____.

_____

_____

(All members of the family sign.)

We, the

_____family,

pledge to serve

__weekly, __monthly, __quarterly

at _____.

_____

_____

(All members of the family sign.)

5.

Extravagant Generosity for Children

Introduction

Fifth-grader Frances Oliver observes with pride as the hairdresser binds her long, flowing hair into a ponytail. She closes her eyes as she feels the first cut of the sharp scissors and opens her eyes to stare at her now short hair. Soon her initial worries and short-lived fear are over when she looks into the mirror at her new fashionable hairstyle. Frances grew her hair long in anticipation of this very moment when she now gives it away.

Last year, when Frances learned her church choir director had been diagnosed with cancer, Frances made up her mind to sacrifice her hair in honor of her. She is happily donating her hair to Locks of Love, an organization that will take her hair and fashion a wig for a cancer patient. The thought that another special lady, one whose name she will never know, will wear a wig made from her hair delights her and humbles her. Frances chose to practice Extravagant Generosity and she presents her gift out of extravagant love and joy for her choir director, the unknown cancer patient, and Jesus Christ.

Fourth-grader Seth Johnson plans a huge birthday bash to celebrate his ninth birthday.

He plans to invite friends from his church and school for a pizza party at his home complete with a soccer-themed birthday cake. Friends honor the request on his invitation, and thus Seth receives no birthday gifts from his friends. Rather, guests bring monetary contributions for a local mission that needs funds. Seth decides he will take the money and give it to the director of the mission himself. His Extravagant Generosity affects several of his friends and they inform their parents that they wish to follow Seth's example at their next birthday party.

Third-grader Lily Thomas receives money from her family whenever she completes chores. She cleans her room, feeds and walks her dog, and helps her family with housework cleaning. The saved money allows her to purchase toys and video games, but before she spends her money on luxuries she sets aside a tithe for her church. She promises to give first priority in her giving to her church as she realizes that God calls her to be a good steward. Lily lives in a family and belongs to a congregation that models and teaches her faithful stewardship. Lily practices Extravagant Generosity in her monetary giving.

How did these children become generous givers? Frances, Seth, and Lily attend churches where they are taught about stewardship. Frances loves her long hair, but chooses to sacrifice it out of extravagant love. Frances learns of God's wonderful grace as she listens to her Sunday school teachers and pastor teach and proclaim the message of God's Extravagant Generosity. Frances's radical gift flows from her thankful heart as she responds to God's abundant generosity and love toward her. Seth learns to practice Extravagant Generosity through lessons on stewardship taught to the children at his church. Lily receives a pledge card and stewardship bag each year from her children's pastor. The bag contains items that help her learn about being a faithful steward. She fills out her pledge card seriously each year and returns it to the church. Lily belongs to a church that welcomes the money offerings of children, and Lily intends to honor her commitment to tithe. All three children practice Extravagant Generosity in their own ways, and God blesses their efforts.

What is Extravagant Generosity? What does it have to do with children?

Our motivation for Extravagant Generosity begins with our picture of God as the Generous Giver. We serve a generous God who reaches to us with love and grace and provides us with abundant gifts. All of our blessings in life are due to God's Extravagant Generosity and kind mercy toward us. God offers us the cherished gifts of family, friends, and a community of faith. God grants us forgiveness, guides us on our life journey, and walks beside us with God's strengthening Presence and continual love. God's faithfulness toward God's children amazes us. We stand in awe when we consider that the Creator of the Universe continually provides for our needs and constantly showers us with protective care.

We serve a Savior who demonstrates extravagant love for us by his willingness to die for us on the cross. Christ's sacrifice for each of us proves his immense love for us. Without Christ's Extravagant Generosity we would remain unredeemed, unsaved, and lost children. Through Christ's humility and obedience we stand as worthy beloved children who rejoice in our salvation. Christ paid the ultimate price on Calvary, and his sacrificial giving causes us to humble ourselves and pledge our allegiance.

God calls each of us to the task of stewardship. Stewardship involves claiming our role as stewards. God intends us to care for all creation and not waste time in careless actions or frivolous spending. When we fail as worthy stewards, we diminish our spiritual relationship with God and God's creation. Yet, when we practice good stewardship, we grow in our faith. Stewardship, like prayer and Bible study, represents a spiritual discipline that matures our faith when we practice it.

Extravagant Generosity flows from a generous heart. We honor our relationship with God and with others when we strive to practice it. We align ourselves with the side of justice and mercy. Paul identifies generosity as one of the fruits of the Spirit and urges Christians to practice it in extravagant ways. Paul teaches us to go out of our way to help a brother or sister in need. Extravagant Generosity changes our lives as we respond to the urging of God's Holy Spirit to step out in faith.

Extravagant Generosity forces us to examine our values. In the midst of a consumer-driven and materialistic society, we center our principles of giving and spending on the standards of God's stewardship. In a world where persons often exhibit selfishness and greed, we seek to demonstrate patience, kindness, faithfulness, and self-sacrifice.

Extravagant Generosity takes many forms. We can generously give our time, our money, and ourselves for service in God's kingdom. Our ultimate goal results in our intention to become tithers, giving ten percent of our earnings to God's work. However, we begin with proportional giving with the goal of tithing. Faithful stewardship requires sacrifices on the part of participants. Some stewards sacrifice eating out in order to honor their tithe. Still others work to lower their credit card debts, consider their borrowing habits, and think seriously about spending habits.

United Methodists follow in the footsteps of the leader of the Wesleyan movement, John Wesley, who teaches us to practice disciplined stewardship. Wesley instructs us to save and give generously. This habit of good stewardship increases the ability of congregations to practice outreach and strengthen the churches. Individuals also make a radical difference in their witness for Jesus Christ when they are faithful stewards.

Children also grow in faith when churches encourage them to become good stewards. Children need lessons on stewardship and help in applying these lessons in their own giving. Many children receive an allowance, so we can teach children to tithe that allowance. Children's ministry teams can put together stewardship bags and give them to the children at the beginning of the church stewardship campaign. These bags offer children items that encourage them to become tithers and explain clearly to them the concept of tithing. Pledge cards allow children to join with adults and youth during the annual church pledge Sunday. Children do not appreciate being left out of important times in the life of the church. Many churches view Stewardship Sunday as an adult day, but children desire to be included as well. Giving children their own pledge cards encourages them to join adults in tithing and stewardship.

God calls each of us to the task of stewardship.

In addition, children learn from biblical lessons that explore the concept of stewardship and provide examples of individuals who practice Extravagant Generosity. Children appreciate adult leaders who not only model for them Extravagant Generosity, but also allow them to participate in situations where they can become fully involved in practicing Extravagant Generosity. Sunday school classes, confirmation classes, and special children's events are avenues to draw children into the meaning and practice of Extravagant Generosity. These venues can not only teach Extravagant Generosity, but also invite children to practice it alongside their church friends.

Children who practice Extravagant Generosity grow in their faith as disciples of Jesus Christ. They learn practices of kindness, compassion, mercy, and love that remain with them throughout their lives. They serve the church and the world as witnesses to God's extravagant love, amazing grace, and life-changing salvation. They serve an extravagant God who expects nothing less than Extravagant Generosity on the part of God's stewards.

Workshop for Lesson Five

Encourage the members of your children's ministry team, your Sunday school teachers, and other volunteers in your children's ministry area to gather for a time of teaching and reflection on the ways children in the church may be involved in acts of Extravagant Generosity.

Prayer and Welcome

Reflections on 1 Samuel 1–3; Malachi 3:1-12

Since these passages are long, divide into teams of three. Give team assignments and ask teams to prepare to come back to the larger group to share.

Team One: Read 1 Samuel, chapter 1.

Have one person take the viewpoint of Hannah's husband, Elkanah. Have one person take the viewpoint of Eli. Have one person take the viewpoint of Hannah. Share what each might be thinking and feeling.

Team Two: Read 1 Samuel, chapter 2.

Have one person read Hannah's prayer. As it is read, have group members write down Hannah's reflections on God and God's actions of justice. Have persons write down how Hannah must have felt each year as she visited her son. Have persons write down what the man of God revealed to Eli.

Team Three: Read 1 Samuel, chapter 3.

Have one person play the role of Eli and one person play the role of Samuel. Have one or more person take the role of the narrator and read the biblical text as Eli and Samuel act out their parts.

Team Four: Read Malachi 3:1-12.

Answer the following questions:
1. Why is God upset with the people at the time?
2. What is a tithe? What was a first-fruit offering?
3. What did God promise the people if they were faithful with their gifts?

Bring the group back together and share. Read for them the Scripture study provided in your curriculum entitled "Focus for the Teacher." Ask the group to relate the Scripture in Malachi to the readings in 1 Samuel.

- Hannah brings Samuel as her tithe to the temple.
- Samuel becomes the first fruit of Hannah's offering.
- Tithing is bringing 10% to God and is the goal of each follower.

- Hannah practices Extravagant Generosity with the gift of her son. Although not a monetary offering, it represents a sacrificial offering.
- Eli mentors Samuel and helps him recognize his call, but he does not keep Samuel from speaking harsh words about his sons. Eli practices Extravagant Generosity by allowing Samuel to fulfill his call from God.
- Samuel practices Extravagant Generosity to the nation of Israel by speaking the truth to them and guiding them back to the ways of the Lord.

Teaching the Children About Extravagant Generosity

Before the workshop time, gather items for stewardship bags for children. Provide bags, money pencils, money erasers, other money items, and the reproducible pledge card and reproducible card on tithing (see page 119). Place these items on a table. Have participants come to the table and put together items for a stewardship bag they could use in their classroom.

After participants put their stewardship bags together, discuss how you will use the bags with the children in your church to teach stewardship.

Invite some leaders in your church, including your pastor, to be present to share their stewardship testimony.

Where to Go From Here?

Get on Board the Steward-Ship

Plan a party for the children. Take time during your workshop to discuss details of the party. Set a date and plan how you will communicate with the children in your church about the party.

Ideas: Transform the room you are using into a ship. Have children walk over a plank to arrive on the ship. Decorate the room with nautical items and have leaders dress as sailors. Give the children sailor hats. Talk about stewardship with the children. Explain what it means. Explain the biblical teaching about tithing. Give the children play money and let them pretend to give the amount they would give if they were tithing. Let them decorate their stewardship bags. Have them put together their own stewardship bags to take with them, which they can fill with items similar to the ones you used in the workshop. Serve cookies decorated with green icing in the shape of a dollar sign.

A Child and Mother Practice Extravagant Generosity

Objective:

The children will:
- Hear 1 Samuel 1:23-28; 2:26; 3:1-19.
- Learn about a child whose mother practices Extravagant Generosity.
- Learn about the call of Samuel.
- Learn ways they can practice Extravagant Generosity today.

Bible Story:

Malachi 3:10a; 1 Samuel 1:23-28; 2:26; 3:1-19: Hannah dedicates Samuel to God. Samuel grows and hears God speaking to him.

Bible Verse:

Now the boy Samuel continued to grow both in stature and in favor with the LORD and with the people.

1 Samuel 2:26, NRSV

Bring the full tithe into the storehouse.

Malachi 3:10, NRSV

Focus for the Teacher

The prophet Malachi instructs the people to "Bring the full tithe into the storehouse" (Malachi 3:10, NRSV). At the time Malachi speaks so forcefully, the people are robbing God by their refusal to offer a tenth of their possessions. They sit in disobedience and greed. Malachi demands that the people turn back to God and make offerings that are pleasing and right. Malachi assures the people of Israel that God blesses them when they are obedient.

Barren Hannah knows of the teachings regarding offerings and takes them seriously. She promises God that when God blesses her with a child she will dedicate the child to the Lord. Hannah fervently and continually prays and eventually she births a son, whom she names Samuel. Rather than a monetary offering, Hannah brings the first fruits of her womb. God instructs the Israelite people to bring their first fruits as offerings to the Lord. She honors her pledge to God. After she weans Samuel, at about the age of three, she takes him to the temple and presents him to the priest Eli. Samuel lives at the temple starting at the young age of three. Samuel serves in God's house until the time he assumes his duties as a prophet.

Modern-day readers sympathize with Hannah. We recognize her great love for her son as she demonstrates this love each year as she returns to the temple at Shiloh for sacrifices. When she arrives, Hannah brings with her a new ministerial robe for her growing son. The robe from the previous year no longer fits him and she sews him a larger one. Samuel wears his mother's gifts as he helps Eli in the temple and keeps the lamps burning.

One wonders if Samuel questions Eli about why his mother and father visit him only once a year and why he is different from other children who live in homes with their families. Surely Eli lets Samuel know that he is a child of worth and a dearly beloved child. No doubt, Eli tells Samuel that his mother's difficult decision to give Samuel to the Lord occurred because God graciously reached out to Hannah, blessed her, and gave her the gift of her son. Hopefully, Samuel realizes that he is a special child, a special blessing, and a special gift from God.

Hannah demonstrates Extravagant Generosity when she presents her son to God for service. She practices tithing, but in an entirely different way than giving her money. Her sacrificial gift is her son, whom she dedicates to the Lord.

Eli the priest mentors Samuel and helps Samuel recognize God's call in his life. The call in the night forces Samuel to acknowledge his future calling as a prophet. Samuel recognizes the serious nature of the call. God asks Samuel to speak challenging words and harsh words directed at the sons of Eli. The text portrays the sons of Eli as evil men who disobey God. Not wishing to hurt Eli, Samuel at first hides the details of his prophetic call. A part of his mission is to speak out against the injustices of Eli's sons, and Samuel fears telling Eli this news. Mentor Eli offers Extravagant Generosity to Samuel when he advises Samuel that he must be true to his call regardless of the consequence or difficulty. Even if Samuel's words hurt Eli, God commands Samuel to speak the truth and Eli agrees that Samuel must obey God. The pivotal part of the story centers in on Samuel's destiny, a destiny he is able to fulfill due to his mother's Extravagant Generosity, his mentor Eli's Extravagant Generosity, and the extravagant, generous call of God.

> **"Bring the full tithe into the storehouse."**
> **(Malachi 3:10, NRSV)**

Hannah practices Extravagant Generosity when she presents her son as a "first fruit" offering at the temple in response to God's Extravagant Generosity toward her. Eli practices Extravagant Generosity when he mentors Samuel, helps him to grow in stature and favor with God and others, recognizes and affirms Samuel's call, and refuses to harbor enmity against Samuel when Samuel condemns the evil actions of Eli's sons. Samuel practices Extravagant Generosity when he ministers to the nation of Israel at a critical time in their history as the people transition from judges to a king. Samuel practices Extravagant Generosity when he speaks prophetic words that draw the people back to God's ways even if he angers the sons of Eli. This cycle of Extravagant Generosity starts when God extends Extravagant Generosity to Hannah and she responds with her "tithe" of sacrificial and generous giving.

Preschool

Extravagant Generosity

Welcome the Children to Extravagant Generosity

Welcome each child by name. Give each child some play money as they arrive. Have the child decorate a small white sack with crayons. Then give each child several dollar symbol cut-outs. Let them glue the cut-outs onto their bags. Have them place their play money in their decorated bags.

Share the Bible Story (1 Samuel 3:1-19)

Gather the children and have them sit on a rug. Read the story of the call of Samuel from a children's Bible or Bible storybook.

Ask the children if they know someone in their church who is like Samuel (acolyte) and Eli (pastor) and serves God.

Reinforce the Story

Provide biblical costumes that might look like the linen ephod (robe) Samuel's mother made for him. Explain to the children that Samuel's mother made a special robe for him to wear and that he was a helper in God's house. His job was to keep the lamps burning. Let the children pretend they are Samuel dressed in their linen ephods.

Set up a table or section of your room and place some candlesticks there. Have a short unlit candle lighter available. If possible, borrow one from your acolytes, if the candle lighter is not too long for the children to use. Let each child pretend he or she is lighting the candles in God's house just as Samuel lit the lamps. Take a picture of each child.

Prepare

Photocopy and cut apart the dollar signs (page 120).

Provide play money, small white sacks, crayons, and glue.

Prepare

Provide a children's Bible or Bible storybook.

Prepare

Provide Bible-times costumes, candles, candlesticks, candle lighter, and camera.

NOTE: Do not actually light the candles.

Play a Bible Game

Set up a place in the room with a sleeping bag or blanket. Have the children sit in a circle. Have one large play money dollar bill. Play music and pass the dollar bill around the circle. When the music stops, the child holding the dollar bill pretends to be Samuel. He or she goes to the sleeping bag or blanket and lies down. Let one of the teachers call out several names, such as "John," "Mary," "Laura," or "Sam," but the child is not to move until he or she hears the name "Samuel." Then he or she is to jump up and join the teacher.

Start the music again, pass the dollar bill, and continue the game until every child pretends he or she is Samuel. Eventually all of the children end up beside the teacher, who calls out the name of Samuel.

Prepare

Provide a sleeping bag or blanket, a large play dollar bill, a CD of praise music, and a CD player.

Practice Extravagant Generosity

Set up a pretend store center in your room. Place items found in your church such as a Bible, a storybook, diapers, toys, a cross, snack food, crayons, markers, and other items the children use in your church or recognize.

Give the children their decorated money sacks, which contain their play money. Let one of your teachers play the role of the storekeeper. Have each child select one item from the store to buy for your church. Take the item to the storekeeper, who will take some of the child's money.

Gather in a circle and have the children show what they bought for the church. Thank them and tell them that people give money at church to help buy things that your church needs. They also give money to help other people buy things they need, such as food, clothes, toys, school supplies, and medicine.

Have the children leave their items on the rug as they go to snack time.

Prepare

Provide items for the store center.

Use the money and money sacks made earlier.

Extravagant Generosity During Snack Time

Invite some of the acolytes in your church to wear their acolyte robes and serve the snack to the children. Remind the children that Samuel helped Eli and acolytes help your church.

Prepare

Invite one or two acolytes to visit.

Provide a simple snack, juice, napkins, and cups.

Be a Cheerful Giver

Remind the children they can bring some money to church. This money helps the church and helps other people. Take the children into the sanctuary. Let them sit on a pew or pews. Give each child coin play money. Let the acolytes who served the snacks to the children pretend to be ushers. Have them pass the offering plates down the pew and let the children put their play money in the offering plate. If your offering plates are too heavy for the children, use baskets.

Go back to your room and show the children the offering box you have wrapped in plain paper. Encourage the children to decorate the box with happy-face stickers. Tell the children that the Bible says, "God loves a cheerful giver" (2 Corinthians 9:7). God wants us to be happy when we give our offerings. Tell the children that they can bring some money to Sunday school and can put it in the offering box when they arrive each Sunday.

Let the children take home their decorated money bags and tell them to bring their offerings to church each Sunday in their bags.

Closing Prayer

Dear God, thank you for Samuel, who helped Eli at church. I am happy I can bring some money to help my church and help others. Amen.

Prepare

Wrap a box in plain paper.

Provide play money coins, offering plates or baskets, and happy-face stickers.

Invite acolytes to help.

Welcome the Children to Extravagant Generosity

Welcome each child by name. As the children arrive give each child a small cardboard box with a small hole cut in the top that money can easily go through. These cardboard boxes may be purchased at craft/hobby stores or online, and some have tops with holes already cut out. Have the children decorate their boxes with money symbols using either money stickers or crayons or markers.

Share the Bible Story (1 Samuel 3:1-19)

Select one child in the class to play the role of Samuel. Have this child lie down on a sleeping bag or blanket. Read or tell the story "Samuel! Samuel!" (page 121). When you say the words "Samuel, Samuel!" have the child lying down jump up and go toward the children. The first two times Samuel gets up, when Eli tells him to go back to bed the children will shout, "Go back to bed!" Samuel will go back to the sleeping bag or blanket and lie down. Continue with the story.

Reinforce the Story

Have some of your acolytes dress in their acolyte robes. Take the children into the sanctuary and let the acolytes show them what their duties are. Some children in your class may serve in this role already.

Explain to the children that Samuel helped Eli in the same way your acolytes help your pastor. Tell the children that Samuel helped Eli in a huge way. Samuel kept the lamps in the temple burning, which was very important. The acolytes help our church in many important ways as well.

Explain the word *extravagant* (something big and huge). Explain the word *generosity* (going out of our way to help another person in need).

Prepare

Provide small cardboard boxes, crayons or markers, and money stickers.

Cut a hole in the top of each box.

Prepare

Photocopy the story "Samuel! Samuel!" (page 121).

Provide a sleeping bag or blanket.

Prepare

Invite acolytes to wear their robes and be class helpers.

Provide chalkboard and chalk, markerboard and markers, or newsprint and markers.

When we put the two words together we have Extravagant Generosity. Write these two words on the board.

Teach the children the word *tithe*. Write the word on the board and have the children say the word several times. Tell the children that God asks us to bring ten percent of our money to help our church, and we call this a tithe. Ask the children if they receive money for chores. Show them what to bring as a tithe if they are given a certain amount of money a week. Older elementary children enjoy figuring this out for themselves.

Extravagant Generosity Scavenger Hunt

Divide the children into several teams of three to five children. Use an adult or youth volunteer to guide each team. Give each child a piece of paper and a pencil. Ask the children to quietly walk around the church and list anything they see that church members gave money to buy. This list might include chairs, supplies in the nursery, supplies in the children's area, acolyte robes, items in the sanctuary, items in the kitchen, and items in the library.

When the children complete their lists, have the team return to the classroom and work together to compile one list. Have one team member read out the team list. After each team finishes their list, have the class shout out, "Thank you, God, for Extravagant Generosity!"

Practice Extravagant Generosity in the Church and World

Encourage the children to bring pennies or change to Sunday school for several weeks. Let the children decide where they could give their money. Offer the children several options of needs in the community or world. Send a note (see page 122) home with parents explaining about the offering of the children and where it will go. Do not make any child feel bad if he or she does not have money to bring. Be sensitive of children who come from homes where they have little money to give. If this fits the majority of the children in your classroom, select another project that does not involve money but still allows the children to reach out to others with Extravagant Generosity.

Prepare

Invite adult or youth volunteers.

Provide pencils and paper.

Prepare

Photocopy the pennies note to send home to parents (page 122) for each child.

Extravagant Generosity Snacks

Have sugar cookies for each child. Have several tubes of green frosting. Let each child decorate his or her cookies with a green dollar sign and then enjoy eating the cookies. Say a thank-you prayer.

Extravagant Generosity in Your Church

Invite the pastor or children's minister to visit your class. Have him or her explain to the children ways the money given in the church is spent within the church and outside the church.

Have children take home their decorated money boxes and encourage the children to put their chore money in the boxes and set aside their tithes to bring to church.

Closing Prayer

Thank you, God, for our story of Samuel, who helped in God's house. Help me to find ways to serve our church. One way I can help is to bring an offering. Thank you for the people at our church who give their money to help our church and other people in need. Help me to become a generous, extravagant giver. In Jesus' name we pray. Amen.

Prepare

Provide sugar cookies, green frosting in tubes, napkins, juice, and cups.

Prepare

Invite a pastor to visit with the children.

Extravagant Generosity

Welcome the Children to Extravagant Generosity

Greet each child by name. Have some math problems for the children to work with a partner. Tell them to figure out 10% of certain dollar amounts. Have these dollar amounts written on newsprint.

Read the Bible Story (Malachi 3:8-12)

Have the children read the Bible story with their partners. Encourage the children to list the reasons God is not pleased with the offering of the people.

Tell them about the teachings in Scripture of bringing first fruits of the people's crops to God and the tithe. Explain to the children that this is like our bringing a tithe or 10% to God. The first fruit comes when we give first to God before we spend our allowance or spending money on other things.

Suggest to the children that they, too, can practice tithing and the giving of their first fruits like Bible people when they set aside 10% of their allowance or spending money and give this first to God before they spend the money on material things.

Look over the math problems you gave the children during the gathering time. Assure them that they now know how to figure their tithe to God.

Reinforce the Bible Story—Tithing Game

Divide the children into two relay teams. Place two offering plates on the table in front of the children. Place some money of differing denominations on a table across the room. Call out different amounts of

Prepare

Provide news-print, markers, paper, and pencils.

Prepare

Provide Bibles, newsprint, and markers.

Prepare

Provide money (in differing denominations) and two offering plates.

money and challenge each child who is at the head of a line to silently decide what the tithe for that amount of money would be. They should quickly run to the table where the money is and grab that amount of money, then run and place it in their team's offering plate.

The first child to the offering plate earns a point for the team if he or she has the correct amount of money for the tithe. Continue this tithing relay race until every child on the two teams has played the game at least once.

The Story of Samuel (1 Samuel 3:1-19)

Read the story of Samuel from the Bible. Some of your tweens will already be familiar with the story. Ask the children to tell you what persons in your church have duties similar to Samuel's (acolytes).

Tell the children of the story of Samuel's mother, Hannah, and the gift of her son to the Lord. Explain to the children that this was Hannah's tithe to God and she gave the fruit fruits of her children to God. Samuel was her first-born son and she presented him to the priest Eli, and so Samuel lived in the temple and served God. Rather than giving her tithe in money form, Hannah gave her son to help the priest Eli. Get the tweens' reaction to this story.

Understanding Extravagant Generosity

Have the tweens look up the words *extravagant* and *generosity* in a dictionary or on a computer. Ask them to brainstorm things they have done in life that were extravagant. Some of these might be:

1. I ate a whole pizza by myself.
2. My family went on a vacation to Europe.
3. I scored the winning run for my baseball team.
4. We had a huge party for my birthday and invited tons of kids.
5. We rented a cabin and went skiing at Aspen.

Have the tweens brainstorm ways they practice generosity. Encourage the tweens to explain how they believe Hannah practices Extravagant Generosity in the Bible story about Samuel.

Have the tweens think about ways Eli the priest practices Extravagant Generosity toward Samuel. *(He lets him live at the temple. He teaches Samuel. He helps Samuel recognize God's call as a prophet. He does not criticize Samuel when he finds out God has instructed Samuel to speak out against the evil actions of Eli's sons.)*

Have the tweens think about ways Samuel practices Extravagant Generosity. *(He helps Eli and lives at the temple instead of his home. He speaks the truth to people in the nation of Israel. He helps the people follow the right ways of God.)*

Explain to the tweens that we practice Extravagant Generosity in our lives because God is a generous God who extends to each of us Extravagant Generosity.

Extravagant Generosity Journals

Give each tween a small journal that you purchase at a hobby, craft, or office supply store. Encourage the tweens to write in their journals ways that God extends Extravagant Generosity to them.

Remind them of the Extravagant Generosity of Christ, who died for each of them. Let the tweens take their prayer journals home and encourage them to look each day for ways God extends Extravagant Generosity to them and write these ways in their journals.

Extravagant Generosity and Tithing

Give each tween a photocopy of your church budget. Divide them into teams of three or four and have each team look at different sections of the budget. Have them report their findings back to the entire group.

Where is the most money in the church budget spent? Where is the least amount of money spent? Remind the tweens that the money for the budget comes from church members, many of whom tithe and practice Extravagant Generosity with their money. Tell the tweens that some of these people give up luxuries so they can give their money to the church.

Extravagant Generosity in the World

Invite the tweens to engage in the practice of Extravagant Generosity. Encourage them to think of a service project they can do for the church to raise money for missions. Share ideas with the tweens about some possible places they could give their money.

Have the tweens plan a project to raise money (bake sale, car wash, chores for church members, and so forth). Get the support of your

Prepare

Provide journals and pencils or pens.

Prepare

Photocopy your church budget for each tween.

pastor, the staff, and the parents of the tweens. Let the tweens make posters to advertise the fund-raising project. Have some tweens write newsletter articles. Invite some tweens to speak in worship. Encourage your tweens to talk about the project in youth and adult Sunday school classes.

Once the tweens raise the money, have your pastor share a prayer of dedication. If the money goes to a local mission, have the tweens deliver the money, tour the mission facilities, and eat lunch together as a group.

Closing Prayer

Thank you, God, for the ways you show us Extravagant Generosity each day of our lives. Thank you, God, for our Bible lessons today about Extravagant Generosity and tithing. Help us to practice Extravagant Generosity in our lives. Help us to practice tithing. Help us to gladly give some of our money to help our church.

Our class is excited about our mission project, which will help us practice Extravagant Generosity. Bless our project and the people we seek to share your love with through the money we will give. We ask our prayer in the name of Jesus, who showed his extravagant love for each person by dying on the cross. Amen.

Families Can Teach Children Extravagant Generosity

Families teach Extravagant Generosity to children when they teach children about a generous, extravagant God who extends generosity to children and their families. Families teach Extravagant Generosity to children when they talk with children about Jesus Christ and his extravagant love for the world. From the circle of God's love and Christ's redemptive grace, families move out to model and practice Extravagant Generosity.

Children learn Extravagant Generosity when parents diligently model this for them. Parents who tithe or give regularly to the church teach children the importance of stewardship. Parents who reject materialistic values and avoid a consumer mentality teach children not to greedily spend and selfishly consume. Parents who save money for necessities rather than spending money on luxuries teach children to be content with what they need and not what they want. Parents who are sacrificial stewards teach children that God owns the world and all blessings are gifts from God. Rather than leading children towards their own selfish interests and the abuse of God's creation, wise parents teach their children to practice justice and generosity toward the world and others.

Suggestions for Ways Families Can Practice Extravagant Generosity

1. Give children an allowance or money for completed chores, but teach them how to tithe this money before they spend any of it for luxuries.
2. Let children take their money to church and place it in the offering plate.
3. Decide as a family what outreach mission projects (beyond your regular offerings) you will support, and let children give some money toward these projects.
4. Encourage your church's children's ministry team to give children their own pledge cards so they can participate along with adults in the annual stewardship campaign of the church.
5. Commit as a family to pledge some of your time to the church to help with needed projects and events. Involve children as volunteers.
6. Teach children about the stewardship of the earth. Practice recycling as a family.
7. Thank God daily for family blessings.
8. Show older children the church budget and talk with them about the way money is spent in the church.
9. Teach older children about the United Methodist connectional system and ways money is used in the local church, the district, the conference, and the world.
10. Teach children about the United Methodist Committee on Relief. When a disaster occurs, give money as a family, but designate it to UMCOR or a trusted agency such as the Salvation Army or American Red Cross.

Stories of Children Practicing Extravagant Generosity

During stewardship season at Trenholm Road United Methodist, Columbia, South Carolina, the children participate in a three- to four-week class on stewardship. They learn what being a good steward entails. They discuss why it is important to give their time, talents, gifts, and service to the church. They also fill out their own ministry menus that allow them to list ways they will serve the church. The children learn that stewardship is more than just money.

Hendersonville First United Methodist, Hendersonville, Tennessee, offers a covenant discipleship group for fifth-graders called Sprouts. During their time together, the children covenant to serve God with acts of kindness and justice and acts of worship and devotion. The Sprouts group decided they wanted to help a program in Hendersonville called Community Childcare. This organization offers quality childcare on a sliding scale based on family income. Many of their children are being cared for in the foster care program or their families require assistance due to lost jobs, going back to school, or other reasons. Community Childcare sought financial help to meet the basic needs of operating and keeping their doors open. The Sprouts group planned and held a carnival that raised money for Community Childcare. The center benefited greatly from the money raised. More importantly, the Sprouts group learned what it means to give extravagantly, not just of money, but also of time, energy, and self. They learned that Risk-Taking Mission and Service helps one grow in his or her faith and their dedicated efforts were worth every moment given.

The children at Haymount United Methodist, Fayetteville, North Carolina, support a young boy in Uganda. The children send him money and write him letters. He in turn writes them back and tells them how he spends the money they send him. At Easter, they gave him an Easter package with stickers, a pencil, paper, and other goodies, and each child made him and his family an Easter card. One Sunday, a third-grade boy brought in an envelope with thirty dollars in it for this young boy in Uganda. He wanted to give this money because he knew the Ugandan boy's birthday was approaching. It turns out that the third-grade boy unselfishly and generously gave his own birthday money to this boy in Uganda.

First United Methodist, Colorado Springs, Colorado, ministers to military families but seeks to teach the children about peace through education. A mission project of the children was to raise money to staff a teacher's position at Muslim schools in Pakistan and Afghanistan, schools where girls were permitted to attend. Their project was "Pennies for Peace Mission." During vacation Bible school, the children raised $5,000. The children were not content with this amount, however. They began to find ways to raise money in the community. Some children sold lemonade, while others collected at the local mall. Three months later, the children had collected $15,000! Then the problem emerged of how to deal with this many pennies. One banker in the church had a bank located close to the church, and he willingly opened his doors on Saturday. The children carried the pennies from the church to the bank in wagons. The operation took five and a half hours.

On the occasion of her last four birthdays, Meri Allen Krueger, a member of Connell Memorial United Methodist in Goodlettsville, Tennessee, instructed the children she invited to her birthday party to bring money for a designated mission. This money was in lieu of any birthday presents for her. One year, Meri Allen gave her money to Room in the Inn, an agency that helps homeless persons in her community. Another year, Meri Allen gave the money to purchase a sound system for the church nursery, so the caregiver could hear the worship service. Meri Allen has also donated money to a friend who was a victim of the recent floods in Tennessee, and she supports her sister, who has arthritis, by sponsoring her walk team, Ana-Carlin's Crew 4 A Cure.

The fifth-grade class at Trenholm Road United Methodist, Columbia, South Carolina, takes two offerings each Sunday. The first is for the church, but the second is for missions. The children hold the responsibility of taking the collection, counting the money, and keeping track of the money. Throughout the year, they learn about different organizations in the community and world. At the end of the Sunday school year, the children discuss and decide where they want their money to go.

Broomfield United Methodist, Broomfield, Colorado, supports Global Hope, a mission endeavor to provide lasting Christian homes for abandoned and orphaned children in Romania and Kenya. The church seeks to teach the children not to simply turn to their parents for money, but to think of creative ways to contribute. One young girl asked her neighbors to allow her to care for their garden by pulling weeds to earn money. She worked diligently for a week to earn an agreed-upon amount, but she earned this money prior to learning about her church's mission project. When she heard about Global Hope, she took all of the money she had earned along with her weekly allowance and donated it to provide milk for the children of Romania.

The fourth- and fifth-graders of Newburgh United Methodist, Newburgh, Indiana, led their congregation in a mission project to raise money to buy water filters for villages in Africa. Ten-year-old Abbey spearheaded the drive. She planned with her church friends "The Purple Toilet Project." Members of the congregation paid to have purple-painted toilets placed on people's lawns, and those individuals had to pay to have them removed from their lawns. "Potty Insurance" ensured that a purple toilet never found its way onto a person's lawn. The children made flyers, and Abbey spoke to the congregation about the project. When the project came to a close after two weeks, the children had raised nearly $2,000, enough to fund four water filters in Africa and pay for part of the plumbing in the Habitat House the church was currently building!

Pledge Card

I can give something to my church and God!

I will give: ____every week   ___every month   ___every year

I can share with my church by:
___attending Sunday school   ___attending worship
___serving as an acolyte   ___participating in the children's choir
___attending VBS   ___attending Kid's Club

Other ways:_____

Name of Child _____

Signature of Parent _____

Tithing Card

I Can Tithe! I can give 10% to God and my church.

HOW???

If I have $1.00—I will give .10
If I have $2.00—I will give .20
If I have $5.00—I will give .50
If I have $10.00—I will give $1.00

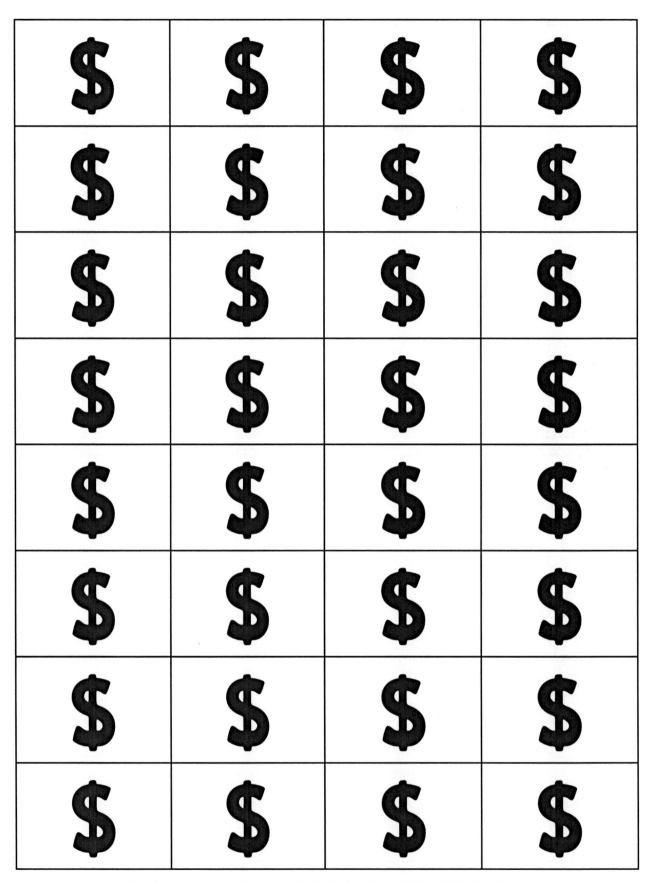

Samuel! Samuel!

Samuel shut the doors to the temple. He checked the oil in the lamp. It was still burning. He took off his coat. Then Samuel spread out his sleeping mat. It was time for bed. Samuel lay down and went to sleep. *(Child lies down on sleeping bag.)*

"Samuel! Samuel!" A voice called to Samuel in the night. *(Child gets up from sleeping bag.)*

Samuel woke up. He thought that Eli the priest had called him. He got up from his sleeping mat and went to the room where Eli was sleeping.

"Here I am," said Samuel sleepily.

Eli woke up. "Why are you here?" he asked Samuel.

"You called me," answered Samuel.

"I did not call you," said Eli. "Go back to bed." *(Children shout, "Go back to bed!")*

Samuel went back to his sleeping mat and lay back down. *(Child lies down on sleeping bag.)* Soon he was asleep.

"Samuel! Samuel!" A voice called Samuel's name again.

Samuel woke up. Again, he thought that Eli the priest had called him. He got up and went to Eli. *(Child gets up from sleeping bag.)*

"Here I am," said Samuel. "I heard you call my name."

"No, I did not call you," said Eli. "Go back to bed." *(Children shout, "Go back to bed!")*

Samuel went back to his sleeping mat. He went back to sleep. *(Child lies down on sleeping bag.)*

"Samuel! Samuel!" A voice called Samuel's name a third time.

Samuel woke up. "Eli must be calling me this time," thought Samuel. He went to Eli. *(Child gets up from sleeping bag.)*

"I am not calling you," said Eli. "You must be hearing the voice of God. Go back to sleep. If the voice calls you again, say 'Speak, Lord. I am listening.'"

Samuel went back to his sleeping mat. *(Child lies down on sleeping bag.)* But he did not go back to sleep.

"Samuel! Samuel!" The voice of God called Samuel's name again.

This time Samuel knew what to do. "Speak, Lord," said Samuel. "I am listening."

Adapted from *BibleZone 4 Preschool,* © 1998 Abingdon Press.

Art: Megan Jeffery

Bring Your Pennies

We are collecting pennies to give to

_____.

Please have your child bring the pennies by

_____.

- -

Art: Megan Jeffery

Bring Your Pennies

We are collecting pennies to give to

_____.

Please have your child bring the pennies by

_____.

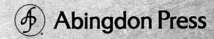

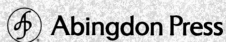

CPSIA information can be obtained at www.ICGtesting.com
Printed in the USA
LVOW091505050313

322834LV00001B/52/P